SCHOLASTIC

Literacy-Building TRANSITION Activities

**Dozens of Quick and Easy Activities
That Infuse Learning Into Every Minute of the Day**

by Ellen Booth Church

D1313846

New York • Toronto • London • Auckland • Sydney
Mexico City • New Delhi • Hong Kong • Buenos Aires

Teaching *Resources*

"Beauty is the moment of transition,
as if the form were just ready to flow
into other forms."

—*Ralph Waldo Emerson*

I would like to thank Deborah Collett Murphy for her
valuable input on the language activities.

Scholastic Inc. grants teachers permission to photocopy material in this book only
for personal classroom use. No other parts of this publication may be reproduced in
whole, or in part, or stored in a retrieval system, or transmitted in any form or by any
means, electronic, mechanical, photocopying, recording, or otherwise, without written
permission of the publisher. For information regarding permission, write to Permissions
Department, Scholastic Inc., 557 Broadway, New York, NY 10012.

Editor: Joan Novelli
Cover design by Jason Robinson
Interior design by Holly Grundon
Interior art by Shelley Dieterichs,
except for pages 12, 14, 16, 27, 28, 36, 39, 41, 45, 64, 67, 72, 83, 93, 96,
97, 98, 117, and 160 by Paige Billin-Frye, Maxie Chambliss, and James Graham Hale.

ISBN-13: 978-0-439-65088-5
ISBN-10: 0-439-65088-7
Copyright © 2008 by Ellen Booth Church

All rights reserved.
Printed in the U.S.A.

1 2 3 4 5 6 7 8 9 10   40   15 14 13 12 11 10 09 08

Contents

Introduction 4

How to Choose and Use Transition Activities 5

Resources 6

Skills Overview 7

10 Tips for Tremendous Transitions 9

Language Arts Transitions 11

Alphabet Recognition 12

Phonemic Awareness 19

Storytelling 33

Word Play 40

Vocabulary 47

Poetry 54

Math Transitions 61

Counting and Estimating 62

Sorting and Classifying 73

Sequencing, Patterning, and Seriating . . . 81

Adding and Subtracting 91

Measuring 100

Graphing 106

Month-by-Month Transitions 112

September 113

October 118

November 123

December 128

January 132

February 136

March 141

April 146

May 151

June 156

Introduction

What is it that makes transition times special? Perhaps it's that they provide a precious opportunity to take a few minutes to do something both meaningful and fun. Or maybe it's the looser structure these times offer, just right for presenting an activity in a brief period of time. Sometimes the best part of any activity is the beginning or end. With transitions it's all beginning and end—there's no time for the middle!

Perhaps we love these mini-activities because they model the big and little real-life transitions we all make day to day. As adults we move from one activity to another several times a day, yet we hardly need to focus on how we do so. In the early childhood years, however, children need to learn how to make these changes and transitions. They need to learn how to shift focus, to pay attention, and to change activities (and moods!) quickly and easily. Our work with transitions in school helps prepare young children for the changes of life.

Of course, this kind of focus and ease with change is not easy to teach. Some of us may actually dread transitions because children can lose control and focus. I remember as a new teacher having moments when I thought I would never regain the children's attention. That's when I discovered that singing a song, or doing a finger play or a dramatic movement, out of the blue could instantly get them looking at me. Then if I engaged them with the activity, too, we were all focused and ready to go on with whatever I had planned.

Most of the activities in this book involve one or more of the arts, such as dance, music, drama, and visual arts. In addition to using the activities as transitions, you can also expand them into longer lessons. The possibilities are endless. Sing a song, do a dance, be dramatic and playful knowing that the learning will happen when children are relaxed, comfortable, and engaged!

It's All About Literacy!

While traditionally we think of language, reading, and writing as "literacy," there are many forms of literacy that young children develop in the early years. In recent years, studies have supported the expansion of the definition of the word literacy to a more overarching term for competence across a variety of skills. The transition activities in each section of this book (language arts, math, and seasonal) are designed to support children's literacy development not only with language, reading, and writing, but also with math, social, physical, and creative skills. The goal in using these activities is to meet the needs of the whole child, encourage children's multiple strengths and intelligences, and provide reinforcement for all of their budding literacy skills.

How to Choose and Use Transition Activities

Activities for transition times come in all shapes and sizes, just like kids! Transitions can be a short interlude or the beginning of something new and bigger. They can be the movement from one event to another. Transitions can provide an opportunity to calm and center children or to use up extra energy in a positive way.

The transition activities in this book are organized into three main sections: Language Arts Transitions (pages 11–60), Math Transitions (pages 61–111), and Month-by-Month Transitions (pages 112–160). You'll find that activities in each of these sections generally fit into one of the following categories:

- Movement from place to place, such as Alphabet Countdown! (page 14)
- Waiting activities, such as The Case of the Missing Pattern (page 89)
- Action breaks, such as Jack, Jump! (page 56)
- Attention grabbers, such as Look at This! (page 129)
- Settling-down activities, such as Cats and Dogs (page 136)
- Thought-provoking times, such as Thinking Caps (page 40)
- Language builders, such as Name Game (page 32)
- Teachable moments, such as Quickly, Quietly (page 52)

> **Teaching Tip**
>
> When possible, model transitions to make it easier for children to successfully follow along themselves.

Many activities naturally combine more than one type of transition—for example, Story Chains (page 34) builds language skills as children move from one place to the next. When choosing activities, consider the type of transition you need at any given time as well as the focus. For example, with Give Me Three! (page 69), children move from one place to another while reinforcing number recognition. A Valentine's Transition Game (page 137) will get them there while they celebrate a special time of the year! For ease of use, activities follow a basic format:

Skills and Concepts: This list highlights key skills supported by each activity.

What to Do: Use these step-by-step directions to guide children in learning-filled transition times—from getting their attention at the start to focusing them on what comes next.

Variations: Put a fresh twist on transition activities with these suggestions. Changing something about an activity while maintaining the general procedure builds children's confidence in their abilities while encouraging them to try new things.

Keep in mind that in addition to the skills identified in Skills and Concepts, activities naturally incorporate other skills. For example, I'm Thinking of a Letter (page 12) reinforces, as identified in the Skills and Concepts list, alphabet recognition, listening, and following directions. As children play, they are also using listening skills, strengthening receptive and expressive language, taking turns, and cooperating with one another. You can also apply skills of your choice to the format of a particular transition. For example, if you are working with students on writing letters, you can incorporate that skill in the transition activity Sound It Out . . . On Your Way Out! (page 30) by inviting children to write their letters on mural paper and create a cooperative art project with them.

Transitions and the Brain

Interestingly, brain research supports the use of transitions as a teaching tool. Studies have shown that the brain pays the most attention to (and remembers best) the first and last thing presented in a lesson. The material in the middle just doesn't engage the mind (and is not remembered) as completely as what's happening on either side of it! When you are using transition time to teach, you are supporting children's natural brain development.

Resources

50 Fun and Easy Brain-Based Activities for Young Learners by Ellen Booth Church (Scholastic, 2002): Engaging activities correlate with current brain-based research to support young children in learning.

The Learning Power of Laughter: Over 300 Playful Games and Activities That Promote Learning With Young Children by Jackie Silberg (Gryphon House, 2004): This practical resource is filled with finger plays, jokes, poems, and more, which are easily adapted for use during transition times.

Phonics From A to Z: A Practical Guide (2nd ed.) by Wiley Blevins (Scholastic, 2006): This comprehensive resource offers practical strategies and lessons for phonics instruction, many of which can be adapted for use as transition activities.

Start Smart by Pam Schiller (Gryphon House, 1999): Playful activities—many just right for transition times—are designed to boost brain development in young children and are accompanied by explanations of how and why they work.

Transition Time: Let's Do Something Different by Jean Feldman (Gryphon House, 1995): Songs, finger plays, games, and stories are organized by typical parts of a school day, such as circle time, clean-up, line-up, and lunch, making it easy to turn transitions from one part of the day to the next into teachable moments.

Skills Overview

The activities in this book support young children in developing a wide range of essential skills. The following chart summarizes skills in five areas: language arts, math, social and emotional, motor, and critical and creative thinking.

Language Arts Skills	Math Skills
Auditory discrimination	Comparing/Sorting
Concepts of print	Concept of zero
Conventions of conversation	Counting
Descriptive language	Number recognition
Inferencing	Estimating
Left-to-right progression	Graphing
Letter recognition	Matching
Listening	Measuring
Matching letters and sounds	More than, less than, equal to
Parts of speech	One-to-one correspondence
Phonemic awareness	Ordering
Receptive and expressive language	Ordinal numbers
Recognizing names	Patterning
Rhyming	Place value
Sequencing	Sequencing
Storytelling	Seriating
Using comparisons	Shapes
Visual perception/discrimination	Spatial relationships
Vocabulary development	Tallying
Word families	Time
Writing	Visual perception

Social and Emotional Skills	Creative and Critical Thinking Skills
Cooperating (teamwork)	Analogies
Decision making	Brainstorming
Focusing attention	Categorizing
Following directions	Classifying
Leadership	Comparing
Relaxation	Creative thinking
Self-esteem	Critical thinking
Sensory awareness	Deductive reasoning
Sharing	Experimenting
Social interaction	Inductive reasoning
Understanding routines	Memorizing
Using imagination	Observing
Motor Skills	Predicting
Eye-hand coordination	Problem solving
Large-motor development	Recognizing attributes
Small-motor development	Reflecting
Spacial relationships	Visual discrimination

10 Tips
for Tremendous Transitions

Consider the following suggestions as you introduce transitions with students.

1 **Create Transition Assistants:** Children are always better at participating in a transition if they have a job to do. Create simple transition assistant jobs such as door opener, snack passer, line leader, line caboose, and clean-up monitor. If possible, make name tags, necklaces, or visors for each of these jobs.

2 **Sing a Song of Praise:** Children always want to hear their name in a song. Just use their names in a simple tune reinforcing a positive behavior. For example, you can sing this phrase to the tune of "The Wheels on the Bus": *I like the way that [child's name] is listening. And I like the way that [child's name] is listening. I like the way that [child's name] is listening. Now we're ready for storytime.*

3 **Use Gerunds:** Short and sweet reminders of appropriate behavior are more effective than all the direction words in the world. Try using one gerund as a quick reminder. If children are starting to run down the hall, you might say, for example, "Walking."

4 **Provide Time to Prepare:** Give children a five-minute, two-minute, and then one-minute warning. Children will have ample time to prepare for a transition if they have plenty of warning. As a group, have children choose a different signal for each of the warning times.

5 **Be Specific:** Simple, short phrases that specify what you want children to do are much more effective than complicated and detailed sentences. Emphasize the important word in the phrase that speaks to what you need them to do, such as *in, out,* and *down.*

6   **Be Surprising:** Just about the time children are getting used to a particular way you are making transitions, change it! Brain research tells us that novelty or change in a particular pattern or sequence will increase children's attention span and engage their thinking.

7   **Model Transitions:** Often, early childhood programs have more than one adult in the classroom. It is extremely helpful if one adult is the transition leader or caller and the other adult acts as a model for the children. This adult can model listening for directions or following directions while encouraging children to join in. Modeled behavior is more powerful and instructive than spoken directions.

8   **Record Music:** Invite children to help you choose music to be used as specific transition reminders or cues. They may like to record an energetic sound for clean-up, some quiet mood music for rest time, and a marching sound for circle time. Change the music frequently to keep interest (and cooperation) high!

9   **Create a "Works-in-Progress" Area:** Children often don't want to transition because they're not finished with something they're doing. Create a shelf area where children can safely place a project that is not complete. Then make time for children to go back to the project at another time. Provide name tags for children to place on their work-in-progress.

10   **Personalize Assistance:** There are always some children who have a difficult time shifting focus. For these children it is best to individually prepare them. Whisper to them that it is almost time to clean up or to move on to the next activity. Ask them to help you get the others ready for the transition or give them a job to do—such as giving the transition or freeze signal. The key is to make children feel involved with the transition!

Language Arts Transitions

Transition time is also language and literacy time! It is the perfect time to introduce, explore, and practice the literacy skills you teach throughout the day. In fact, these literacy mini-lessons can be an essential part of your literacy program. They provide children with the opportunity to apply the skills they're learning in the classroom to "real life" experiences—thus demonstrating to children how literacy skills are something they use not only in school but everywhere!

You can use literacy transitions to quiet the group and gain children's attention, move them from place to place, provide a creative break in the action, or constructively fill waiting time. In addition to providing needed structure for transitions, the activities in this section reinforce skills, develop new ones, and build memory and retention. (See pages 7–8 for a comprehensive list of skills.)

As you choose transition activities to use with children, keep in mind the importance of repetition. The more you use a particular transition, the more children gain understanding. So have fun exploring a transition for a while and then switch to another. But remember to revisit the transitions throughout the year as a way of assessing children's understanding, expanding their thinking, and building their confidence as learners!

Section Organizer

The transition activities in this section are grouped by the following topics:

Alphabet Recognition (pages 12–18)

Phonemic Awareness (pages 19–32)

Storytelling (pages 33–39)

Word Play (pages 40–46)

Vocabulary (pages 47–53)

Poetry (pages 54–60)

I'm Thinking of a Letter

Skills and Concepts

- listening
- letter recognition
- following directions

Play an alphabet game that transitions children two by two to the next activity.

 What to Do

1. Ask a letter question using this example as a model: "Banana, ball, billboard, beach . . . what letter am I thinking of?"

2. Children raise hands and the child who answers correctly invites a partner to say one more word that starts with the same letter.

3. Together, these children move to the next activity. Continue transitioning children in this way by twos to the next activity.

Teaching Tip

Including letter recognition activities throughout the day helps reinforce children's knowledge of the alphabet, an essential prerequisite for learning to read.

Variations

 Add an Alphabet Chart: Add an alphabet chart for added work with visual discrimination of letters. When you ask the question "What letter am I thinking of?" children have to identify the letter on the chart and name it.

 Reverse It! Say the letter and give the description of something that starts with the sound. Ask children to guess what it is. The child who guesses correctly invites a partner to name another object whose name begins with the same letter.

Conduct the Alphabet!

Skills and Concepts

- letter recognition
- concepts of print
- following directions

Young children love to experiment with "air writing," the process of writing and drawing with a finger in the air! Expand their fun by making simple batons for conducting the alphabet letters. Then play a game that lets children air-write letters as they transition to new activities. Prepare batons in advance so they are ready to use during transition times. (See Teaching Tip, below right.)

What to Do

1. Discuss with children how a symphony works and how a conductor uses a baton to direct the musicians.

2. With batons in hand, have children practice "conducting" letters of the alphabet. Starting with *A*, model how to use the baton (knob facing out) to slowly draw the letter in the air. Repeat with other letters.

3. Once children have practice with this technique, use the baton to play a guessing game. Draw a letter with a baton and have children follow your motions with their own batons. What letter is it?

4. Excuse children from the group who correctly identify the letter. (Children can whisper the letter to you if you do not want them to call out.) Eventually children can be the conductor for this alphabet transition.

Teaching Tip

To make batons, have children decorate paper towel tubes (with crayon and markers, or by gluing on scraps of colorful paper and ribbon), and then stuff tissue paper in one end to create a knob.

Variations

- **Use Children's Names:** Use a baton to conduct children's names and excuse them from the group or call them to circle time.

- **Sing a Song:** Together, conduct the letters as children sing the alphabet song. It will add an auditory clue to identifying the letters! This is a good activity for filling a few extra minutes. Or try this while you are moving from one place to another. Children's attention will stay focused ahead on the baton.

Alphabet Countdown!

Have you ever noticed how children will hurry up and do something, such as line up, when you give them a countdown? There is something fun about a race against time. Children often will get going faster (and better) for a countdown than when given all the reminders in the world!

Skills and Concepts

- letter recognition
- following directions
- listening

What to Do

1. Ask students: "Do you think we can get ourselves lined up before the end of the alphabet song? Sing it with me to see!"

2. Sing the alphabet song to "count" how long it takes to get lined up. Notice with children what letter they were on when they finished lining up.

3. Each time you use the alphabet song for this particular transition (or for others, such as cleaning up or sitting down), have children notice how far through the alphabet they went. Encourage children to do it faster next time.

Variations

- **Add an Alphabet Chart:** Use an alphabet chart to add visual letter recognition and recording skills to the activity. Make a vertical chart of the letters, starting with *Aa* at the top and ending with *Zz* at the bottom. Leave room to the right of each letter to check off how far into the song children get before the transition is complete. You can even date each entry to keep track of progress!

- **ABC Order:** To reinforce letter recognition and sequence, make a set of alphabet cards. Give one to each child as you prepare to line up. Sing the alphabet song as children arrange themselves in ABC order. Repeat the song until all children are in line.

Stick It to Me

A sticky note in the hand signals young children to leave circle time and focuses their attention as they transition to their next activity.

Skills and Concepts

- letter recognition
- matching letters and sounds
- recognizing uppercase and lowercase letters

What to Do

1. Write letters on sticky notes (one letter per note). As children leave circle time, place a sticky note in the palm of each one's hand.

2. When children receive their sticky notes, they look around the classroom to find an object whose name begins with their letter's sound.

3. When children think they have found a match, they place the sticky note on the object. Check to see if a correct match has been made. (You may wish to write children's names on one side of the sticky note to assist with assessment.)

Variations

• **Sticky Note Match:** Hide a second set of sticky notes (with letters on them) around the classroom and have children match the sticky notes they have on their palms to the hidden ones. They can match lowercase to lowercase, uppercase to uppercase, or, if appropriate, lowercase to uppercase.

• **Letter Box:** Instead of sticky notes, use alphabet cards, letter tiles, or magnetic letters. Place them in a box and let children choose their letter at random.

Keys to the Castle

A simple prop makes all the difference in a transition—catching children's attention and sparking their imagination. Of course, once you "have them" you can use the transition to teach any number of literacy skills. Try this one to inspire letter and sound learning.

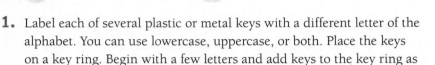

Skills and Concepts

- letter recognition
- matching letters and words
- visual discrimination
- creative expression

 What to Do

1. Label each of several plastic or metal keys with a different letter of the alphabet. You can use lowercase, uppercase, or both. Place the keys on a key ring. Begin with a few letters and add keys to the key ring as children develop skills and knowledge.

2. When children are waiting in a line, give the key ring to the first child and say, "These are the keys to a castle."

3. The child chooses a key—for example, *Kk*—pretends to open the door to a castle, and then says, "In my castle there is a *K* room and inside there is a king." If it is too difficult for children to suggest a word that begins with this letter, you can offer suggestions. This modeling will help children understand the game and enable them to add the word during a repetition of the game at another time.

4. The child then passes the key ring to the next child in line, who chooses a key to another "room in the castle." (Depending on how much time you have for the transition, children can repeat letters, or you can repeat the transition at other times, making sure to give a different group of children a chance each time.)

Teaching Tip

Prior to these activities, ask questions about the different environments to stimulate children's thinking—for example, "What is a castle? Who lives there? What do they do?"

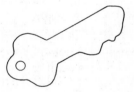

Variations

- **Keys to the Zoo:** Use the keys to open the gates to a zoo. Example: "These are the keys to a zoo. In my zoo there is a *T* area and in that area there is a tiger."

- **Keys to the Supermarket:** Use the keys to open the door to a supermarket. Example: "In my supermarket there is a *B* shelf and on that shelf are bananas."

- **Keys to the Department Store:** Use the keys to open the door to a big department store. Example: "In my department store there is an *S* shelf and on that shelf there are shirts."

Alphabet Airlines

Ask children if they have ever seen an airplane make messages in the sky. Let children share their stories, and show them pictures of skywriting, if possible. As children wait in line for a transition, try some writing in the sky that reinforces following directions.

Skills and Concepts

• letter recognition
• handwriting
• large- and small-motor development

 **What to Do**

1. When children are lined up, have one child step forward to be Captain of the Alphabet Airlines. Announce the captain in this way: Captain Tanya is the pilot of the *T* Airlines and her airplane is going to make a *T*. (Substitute names and letters to correspond to individual children.) Invite this child to stand with you to lead the class.

2. Have children hold the arm they use for writing straight out in front of them, level with their shoulder.

3. Give verbal directions on how to form the letter while modeling it (along with the captain) in the air. Face in the same direction as the children so they are forming the letter correctly. You might say, "This is your pilot, Captain Tanya. Together, we're going to make the letter *T*. To make a *T*, reach way up high in the sky and then move your arm straight down. Now reach up and over to the left and fly straight across to the right. Then bring your arm back down to your side."

4. Continue with other letters, having children take turns stepping forward to be Captain of the Alphabet Airlines.

Variations

⊚ **Wiggle Worm Writing:** Have children write letters in the air with just their index finger. Without naming the letter, model how a letter is formed. (Be sure you're facing the same direction as the children.) While you write, sing the following to the tune of "I'm a Little Teapot": "I'm a little wiggle worm, short and fat. Here is my letter. What letter is that?" Have children try to guess the letter they are making.

⊚ **Do a Letter Dance:** As children line up, call out letters and have them "write" them on the floor with their toes. This little dance will make standing in line a learning experience.

Alphabet Soup

Need something comforting for a transition to lunchtime? How about a bowl of alphabet soup? It's fun and easy and requires just a few props.

Skills and Concepts

- letter recognition
- observing
- taking turns
- small-motor development

What to Do

1. Collect a big soup pot, a medium soup bowl, a large wooden spoon or ladle, and a set of letters (magnetic letters or plastic tiles or cubes). Place the letters in the pot.

2. Invite each child to take a turn stirring the letters in the pot (the alphabet soup). As the child stirs, everyone chants, "Alphabet, alphabet, alphabet SOUP!" On *soup*, the child picks out a letter, names it, and then places it in the soup bowl.

3. That child then leaves to get ready for lunch, and the next child takes a turn. This continues until all children have stirred the soup and are ready for lunch.

Variations

- **Lunch-box Letters**: Change the context of the game, using a lunchbox (or lunch bag) theme instead of the soup pot. Place letters in a lunchbox. As a child shakes the lunch box, everyone chants, "Lunch, lunch, what will we munch?" Then the child opens the lunch box, chooses and names a letter, places it on a tray or plate, and then proceeds to get ready for lunch.

- **Alpha-Ade**: Place letters in a pitcher. Let children take turns stirring the "alpha-ade" as everyone chants, "Stir, stir, stir the drink. What's this letter, do you think?" Children use a long-handled spoon to scoop out a letter, then name it, place it in a tall cup, and move on to get ready for lunch.

Rhyme Me

In this game, children have to rhyme along with you. There is an excitement that builds as children chime in with rhyming words. Best of all, children have to listen carefully to one another and work together to keep this game going. By the time you are ready to transition to the next activity, you will have a calm, focused, and cohesive group!

 What to Do

1. To play the game, tell children they have to listen for the ending sound of a word and choose a new beginning sound to go with it. Share an example using the following format: "If I say *rug* . . . you say _____." (*bug, dug, hug*) Invite children to suggest both make-believe and real words. They will be using phonemic awareness skills no matter what!

2. Substitute any easy-to-rhyme word (in place of *rug*), and repeat: "If I say *hat* . . . you say _____ ." (*sat, cat, bat*) Let children take turns suggesting words. Repeat with new rhyming words as time allows.

Skills and Concepts

- listening
- phonemic awareness
- rhyming
- word families

Teaching Tip

Research shows that teaching phonemic awareness, including through rhyming games, increases reading and spelling achievement. (Ball & Blachman, 1991; Lundberg, Frost, & Peterson, 1988; and Yopp, 1992, as cited in Blevins, 2007)

Variations

- **Rhyme and Write:** Play this game in an auditory mode for quite some time before writing down any of the words. Eventually you will want to write the words on chart paper so children can see the similarities and differences in the words. This is a great introduction to word families!

- **Silly Sentences:** Children can use the rhyming words from the game to create their own funny sentences: "The rug rolled on the bug and gave it a hug!"

A Sack of Rhyming Stories

Fill a pillowcase or bag with objects that have rhyming names and use for this group pass-along story game! Keep your rhyming bag stocked so that it's ready to go whenever you need a calm and centering break.

Skills and Concepts

- rhyming
- storytelling
- phonemic awareness
- taking turns

What to Do

1. Gather a set of objects (or pictures of objects) with names that rhyme, such as *cat*, *hat*, *bat*, *rat*, and *mat* or *ring*, *swing*, *spring*, and *string*.

2. To play, pull out an object and start a sentence about it: "The *cat* was looking out the window one day when . . ." Pass the bag to a child who removes another object and continues the story: ". . . he saw a *bat* fly by!" Continue passing until the group has created a story using all the objects.

Variations

- **The Cat Is Back!** To keep the story going and involve more children, return objects to the bag once they've all been used, and use them again to add on to and embellish the story.

- **Gnat, Chat, Scat:** Extend the fun and learning by asking children to brainstorm more words that rhyme with other words in their story. Write these on chart paper and invite children to use them to keep the story going!

Calling All Rhyming Pairs!

Use pairs of rhyming words to transition children two by two from one activity to another.

Skills and Concepts
- rhyming
- listening
- following directions
- phonemic awareness

What to Do

1. Place picture cards in a bag or box.

2. Invite the first child to draw a card and name the object in the picture—for example, *dog*.

3. Whoever can suggest a real or pretend rhyming word for that word (*dog*) becomes that child's partner and they move on to the next activity. Repeat until all children have transitioned. For an odd number of children, let one group transition by threes. (In this case, two children will suggest a rhyming word for the picture card another child selects.)

Variations

- **Picture Pairs:** Make it a rhyming-pair card game! Paste pictures of rhyming pairs on 3- by 5-inch cards. (Old workbooks are a good source of pictures.) Give each child one card. Have one child tell what is pictured on his or her card. Then ask who has a picture card that makes a rhyme. The children with a rhyming pair of cards repeat their words for others to check and then transition from the group.

- **Cap and Map:** Use objects instead of cards. Gather pairs of objects with names that rhyme and give one to each child. Let children transition with their partners when they find their matches. Children will love to carry their rhyming pair objects with them to snack time or wherever they are going. Sample object pairs: cap/map, string/ring, dice/mice (toy), bread (from the dramatic play center)/thread (spool), black (crayon)/sack, dot (on paper)/knot, rock/sock.

Thinking of Something

Skills and Concepts

- listening
- rhyming
- vocabulary development

Play a rhyming riddle version of the game "I'm Thinking of Something" at snack time or as part of transition time. As children practice listening skills they will also be strengthening phonemic awareness skills.

 What to Do

1. Select a word that children can easily rhyme, such as *cat*. Complete the following riddle frame with the word and a clue about the word: "I'm thinking of something that rhymes with _____ and [give a clue]. What is it?" (or "Who is it?") Begin with easy words, increasing the difficulty over time. Examples:

   - I'm thinking of something that rhymes with *cup* and is a name for a baby dog. What is it? (*pup*)

   - I'm thinking of something that rhymes with *bread* and is part of your body. What is it? (*head*)

   - I'm thinking of something that rhymes with *chairs*, and they are friends to Goldilocks. Who is it? (*bears*)

   - I'm thinking of something that rhymes with *cracker* and is a funny name for a duck. What is it? (*quacker*)

2. Let children guess the word, then repeat with a new word and clue. As children become familiar with the structure of the riddle, they can take turns sharing their own.

Variations

🌀 **Sights and Sounds:** Take this game outside for a walk. Use the sights and sounds of the environment as a source of rhyming words. For example you might say: "I am thinking of something that rhymes with *beef* and grows on a tree. What is it?" (*leaf*)

🌀 **Initial Sound Riddles:** Instead of rhyming words, give beginning sounds and clues. For example: "I'm thinking of something that begins with /b/ and sails on the water. What is it?" (*boat*)

A Fat Cat Run-On Sentence!

Skills and Concepts

- rhyming
- word families
- creative expression
- following directions

When is a run-on sentence an acceptable language form? When it is part of a transition activity that gets children playing with rhymes and word families.

What to Do

1. Start out a sentence with a few words from the same word family (-*at*, -*op*, etc.), and then invite children to keep the sentence going using rhyming words. For example, you might say: "The fat cat sat on a _____. Who can add a word that rhymes with *fat* and *cat*? Remember, made-up words are A-OK!"

2. Add children's suggestions to the sentence as you repeat it: "Yes, the fat cat sat on the rat with a bat that then said *zat!*"

3. Encourage children to keep the sentence going by asking "What else can we add? What other words rhyme with _____? What can we add to make this the longest sentence ever?"

Variations

Fat Cat Chart: It is helpful to have an alphabet chart nearby to record the words in the run-on sentence as it is being constructed. This list can become a rhyming resource for other classroom activities.

Paper-Chain Sentences: Record the sentences children make on paper strips (one word per strip), and then link them together to make a paper chain. Display so children can revisit their sentences and compare the length of new sentences each time they repeat the activity.

Sing It, Rhyme It!

Songs and rhyming are a natural combination, and a perfect activity when children need a change-of-pace transition.

Skills and Concepts

- rhyming
- vocabulary development
- listening
- sequencing

What to Do

1. Choose a familiar song, such as "This Old Man" (see right).

2. As you sing the song with children, leave off the second in each pair of rhyming words and let children chime in to complete the phrase—for example, "This old man he played three, he played nick-nack on my _____." The real word is *knee* but children might suggest *tree, flea,* or *bee.* Try them all to see how each word changes the "story" of the song.

Teaching Tip

Many song phrases end with rhyming words. Strengthen both listening and rhyming skills by leaving off the last word of a phrase for children to "sing-in."

"This Old Man"

This old man, he played one,
He played nick-nack on my thumb,
With a nick-nack patty-wack, give your dog a bone,
This old man came rolling home.

This old man, he played two, … on my shoe, …
This old man, he played three, … on my knee, …
This old man, he played four, … at my door, …
This old man, he played five, … on his tie, …
This old man, he played six, … on some sticks, …
This old man, he played seven, … up to heaven, …
This old man, he played eight, … at my gate, …
This old man, he played nine, … on a dime, …
This old man, he played ten, … once again, …

Variations

- **Expand on the Song:** What would happen if there were more verses to the song? What would they be? Expand children's rhyming skills by asking them to suggest rhymes for the verses (and numbers) 11 through 20 of "This Old Man"! Remember that made-up rhyming words are just as wonderful as real ones because the focus is on hearing the sound that matches. What rhymes with twenty? *(Plenty!)*

- **More Rhyming Songs:** Try another variation on a rhyming song: "I'm Being Swallowed by a Boa Constrictor!" What other body parts can it swallow? "Oh dinger, he swallowed my finger!" Use a simple diagram of the human body to inspire children's verses and to teach content vocabulary.

Rhymon Says

Most children know how (and love) to play Simon Says. Perhaps part of the fun is getting "caught" by Simon doing the wrong movement. It can also be that children take to the lighthearted competition with themselves rather than with others. You can use the Simon Says game structure to practice rhyming words and sounds.

Skills and Concepts

• rhyming
• auditory discrimination
• listening
• following directions

What to Do

1. In advance of playing "Rhymon Says" as a transition activity, introduce children to the traditional version of Simon Says. In the early childhood years it is best to let children laugh when Simon catches them in a mistake instead of making them leave the game. This allows them to enjoy the fun of the game without worry of making mistakes.

2. At a transition time, introduce the Rhymon Says version. Explain that as the leader, you will be saying two words. If the words rhyme, children touch their head and nod to indicate "yes." If the words do not rhyme, children wag their finger and shake their head "no." For example, say: "Rhymon says, 'hot and pot.'" (*Children touch their head and nod "yes."*) "Rhymon says, 'tag and sag.'" (*Children touch their head and nod "yes."*) "Rhymon says, 'fish and frog.'" (*Children wag their finger and shake their head "no."*)

Variations

• **Hot, Pot, Dot:** For a challenge, say three words. If they all rhyme, children touch their head and nod to indicate "yes." If they don't all rhyme, children wag their finger and shake their head "no."

• **Rhymon Says, "Add a Word!"** Eventually children will be able to add another word to the rhyming string. So if Rhymon says "hat" and "pat," children respond "cat!" If Rhymon says two words that do not rhyme, children can again wag their finger and shake their head "no."

Sound Waves

Using letter sounds in playful ways provides important practice and motivates children's interest in learning to read. This lively transition encourages children to work as a team and reinforces vowel sounds.

Skills and Concepts

- phonemic awareness
- cooperating
- creative expression

What to Do

1. Have children stand in a line. Show them how to bend at the waist so their arms are dangling in front of them.

2. Demonstrate by making a vowel sound, such as long *a*. As you do so, stand tall and raise your arms over your head, waving them side to side. Let children say the same sound and practice the same movement.

3. Have the first child (beginning at either end of the line) make a vowel sound, then stand tall and raise his or her arms up, waving them from side to side. The second child then "picks up" the same vowel sound, stands tall, and waves his or her arms skyward. This continues until the sound rolls down the line and everyone has their arms high and waving!

Variations

○ **Reverse the Wave:** You can then start from the end of the line with a new sound and everyone rolls back down one by one. You can keep going back and forth with each new vowel sound so it becomes a smooth wavelike movement.

○ **In a Circle, In Your Seat:** Perform the same exercise standing in a circle or seated in rows.

○ **ABC Wave:** Use all the letters of the alphabet instead of just vowel sounds.

In My Grandmother's Trunk

Skills and Concepts

- phonemic awareness
- memorizing
- taking turns
- letter recognition

For children to be able to identify and match letters and sounds, they need to practice in a variety of ways. Transition time is perfect for a mini-lesson in naming letters.

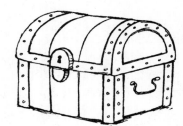

What to Do

1. Use a suitcase, an old-fashioned trunk, or a cardboard box made to look like a trunk. Place it in the center of the circle at meeting time. In another container, place plastic letters.

2. As each child gets up to leave the circle, he or she chooses a letter from the container and then completes this sentence: "In my grandmother's trunk there is a [letter name]." The child then places the letter in the trunk and moves out of the circle and on to the next activity.

3. Each child follows in turn, repeating the previous letters and adding the new letter. To simplify the activity, have children repeat only the letter of the child before her and then add her own. Children can try to repeat more letters as they are able.

Variations

- **Pack a Picture:** Use pictures that represent concrete words, such as *dog*, *cat*, or *apple*. Have children choose a picture, say the word, and then complete the sentence with the word or the first letter of the word.

- **B for Block:** Fill the container with actual items that start with letters that children know. Each child then takes out an item—for example, a block—and says, "In my grandmother's trunk there is a *b* for *block*." Have children repeat only the letter and item that came directly before theirs, or more if they choose.

- **Letter Trunks:** Label a small box or "trunk" for each letter of the alphabet. As children choose a letter, they match it to the corresponding trunk, chanting, "In my grandmother's [letter name] trunk there is a [something that begins with that letter]."

I Know a Fat Frog . . .

Got a few minutes to fill, or need a fun, quieting activity before transitioning to something else? Use a favorite song to inspire some new lyrics and phonemic awareness practice. Children love creating variations on songs because the process allows them to take something they are familiar with and follow the pattern to create something new. This is creative linguistic thinking at its best!

Skills and Concepts

* phonemic awareness
* sequencing
* creative thinking
* listening

 ## What to Do

1. Together, sing the traditional song "There Was an Old Lady Who Swallowed a Fly."

2. Ask, "What if the lady in the song was a fat frog who only swallowed things that started with the /f/ sound?" Sing a new version of the song to demonstrate:

   > I know a fat frog that swallowed a fish.
   > I don't know why he swallowed a fish.
   > What a silly dish!

3. Have children brainstorm all kinds of logical and illogical things that start with *f* that the fat fish could swallow. For example, he could eat a *flower, fan, fruit, figs, feather,* and *football.* The sillier the better!

4. Sing new verses using children's words. At the end of the song add a line such as:

   > I know a fat frog that swallowed a fish.
   > He's FULL, of course!

Teaching Tip

Share one of the many children's book versions of the song to illustrate the process—for example, the eye-catching Caldecott Honor–winner *There Was an Old Lady Who Swallowed a Fly* by Simms Taback (Viking, 1997).

Variations

- **Letter Lists:** As children suggest the words, write them on chart paper to help students make sound-symbol connections, provide reference for their writing, and create "read-the-room" resources.

- **Silly Song Book:** Write each new verse along the bottom of sheets of art paper and have children illustrate. Put the pages together to create a class Big Book.

Alliterative Tongue Twisters

Skills and Concepts

• phonemic awareness
• expressive language
• creative thinking
• listening

Most children are fascinated with the sounds of words and the structures of language. In the early years they begin to enjoy riddles, jokes, and tongue twisters. The best part is that a joke doesn't even have to be funny. If children say it is a joke, it is a joke. Transition times are perfect for exploring letter sounds with tongue twisters.

What to Do

1. Introduce a target letter, such as *b*, and invite children to brainstorm words that start with the letter sound. Encourage them to look around the classroom for ideas.

2. Record the words children suggest, then put the words together to create a tongue twister. For example, "Block, button, banana, ball, baby bottle." Can children say it three times fast?

Teaching Tip

You might want to bring in some objects that start with the target letter to inspire the first few rounds of this game. For the letter *b*, for example, fill a bag or pillowcase with a block, a button, a banana, a ball, and a baby bottle. Invite children to reach in the bag and name the item they pull out. Then put all the words together to make a tongue twister.

Variations

🌀 **Silly Sentences:** Rather than listing words beginning with the target letter to make the tongue twister, combine them in a sentence, adding other words as necessary to complete the sentence.

🌀 **Letter Hunt:** Label bags with target letters. Let teams of children go on a hunt in the classroom for objects that go in the bag. Have them use the names for their objects to make tongue twisters to share with the class.

Sound It Out . . . On Your Way Out!

Skills and Concepts

- phonemic awareness
- letter recognition
- auditory discrimination

As children begin to learn how to sound out letters and words, they delight in sounding out anything and everything around them! Use their interest to create a silly and fun way to make a phonemic exit from a group activity.

  ## What to Do

1. Use alphabet cards or blocks to practice letter sounds as a transition from circle time. Fill a bag or pillowcase with letter cards or blocks. It is helpful to limit the selection to letter sounds children are learning.

2. Invite children (one at a time) to reach in the bag, pull out a letter, and then name it and make the corresponding sound.

3. For every few children, pause and let them put their letter sounds together to make a nonsense word—for example, the letters *p*, *f*, and *t* make *pft*. These children are then excused from the group and go on to the next destination chanting their new word! (Children may return their letter cards or blocks to the bag depending on how many letters and children you have.)

Variations

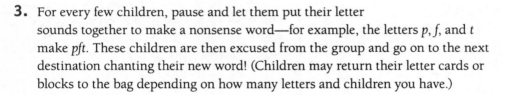

One by One: As children select a letter from the bag, have them name it, say its sound, and then (if they're ready) say a word that begins with that sound. Children then exit the group one by one.

Magnetic Letters: Use magnetic letter titles instead of letter cards or blocks. Have children place their letters on a magnetic board, arranging them in alphabetical order as they go.

Sounds All Around

Skills and Concepts

• phonemic awareness
• auditory discrimination

It's important for children to take a skill they used in one activity and apply it in another similar but different activity. This builds the higher-order thinking skills of application and synthesis. For an interesting extension, try A Symphony of Words (see page 47).

What to Do

1. Discuss with children how a symphony works and how a conductor uses a baton to direct the musicians.

2. Use a drumstick or a wand as a baton to demonstrate, conducting children as they start and stop their voices, their vocal instruments. First, encourage children to make any noise they can all together. Signal them to stop with a wave of the baton. Then have them make letter sounds by asking questions to provoke a variety of sounds as you use the baton to conduct their answers. For example, ask, "Can you make the sound of a clock?" ("Tick, tock, tick, tock.") "What sound do you hear at the beginning?" ("/t/") "What letter makes that sound?" ("*T! T! T!*")

3. Repeat with other sounds, such as for a cat, bell, or zipper.

Variations

🌀 **Sounds All Around:** Ask children to close their eyes and listen to the sounds they hear in the room or outside while they are lining up. Ask them to name the source of the sound (such as a door) and say the matching letter sound. Use the baton to direct the children's participation.

🌀 **Sites and Sounds:** Have children create sounds that would be found in specific environments. Ask: "What kinds of sounds might you hear at a farm?" or "What might you hear at a construction site?" Have children offer different examples by creating and naming the sounds and saying the initial letter and sound.

Name Game

Invite children to join the group or excuse them from a group activity with an alliterative phrase that features their name.

Skills and Concepts

• phonemic awareness
• descriptive language

What to Do

1. Introduce alliteration: the same letter sound at the beginning of adjacent or closely positioned words. Provide examples to show how fun it sounds when the beginning sounds of words are the same—for example, "Bouncing, bubbly Bobbie" or "Delightful, dancing dog."

2. Together create an alliterative chant that features each child's name (or pairs or trios of names that begin with the same letter). Include movement words for added fun.

3. Use the chant to invite children to make their entrance or exit—for example, "Happy, hopping Henry" or "Wildly waving Wanda."

Variations

● **Whose Clue?** Provide alliterative clues to help children guess the name of the child who could fit that description—for example, "I am thinking about smiling, singing _____, who needs to come to our circle."

● **Meet Our Creative, Clever Class!** Have children illustrate their alliterative name phrases for an innovative class album.

Every Sound Tells a Story

Skills and Concepts

- listening
- auditory discrimination
- sequencing
- storytelling

When you have a few minutes between activities, use the sounds around you to start a story. Depending on where you are, you might hear an airplane passing overhead, a cat meowing, a car starting, children making their way down the hall, or a host of other sounds. As children focus their attention on the sounds around them, their story will take shape.

What to Do

1. Invite children to close their eyes and listen. Guide their listening by asking questions such as:

   - What do you hear?

   - What do you imagine is happening?

   - What might happen next?

   - Can we tell a story about what you hear?

2. You might want to start the story yourself using the images and events suggested by children. Then invite children to join in the process and extend the story, incorporating new sounds as they hear them.

Variations

🌀 **Story Charts:** Extend the activity by recording children's stories on chart paper, one sentence per line. Cut the story into strips (by sentences) and let children illustrate each one. Put illustrations and sentences together in a Big Book format that students can revisit on their own.

🌀 **Sound Samples:** Children might want to go on a "sound recording" hunt around the classroom, playground, and school. They can use a tape recorder to collect sound samples to bring back to class and use for storytelling activities.

Story Chains

Pictures of people (and animals, if desired), places, and vehicles prompt imagination-filled story chains that turn a transition from circle time into a literacy-rich experience.

 What to Do

1. In advance of using this activity, have children cut out pictures from magazines of people, animals, places, and vehicles. Place each set of pictures in a separate shoebox. Place the picture boxes in the center of the circle.

2. Select a picture from each box and use them to begin a story—for example, "Once upon a time there was a _____ named _____ [person or animal]. One day she went _____ [place] in her _____ [vehicle]."

3. One at a time, each child adds on to the story, and then leaves the circle. For example, children can elaborate on where the traveler went and why, how long it took to get there, sites the traveler saw along the way, or things that happened.

4. Choose new pictures along the way to introduce new characters or other elements to the story.

Teaching Tip

Introduce and practice the skill of retelling. Later in the day, revisit the story children created. Invite them to recall and retell as many details of the story as they can. Ask questions to encourage sequencing skills—for example, "And then what happened?" "What happened next?" "What happened after that?"

Variations

- **Everyone Picks a Picture:** Choose a picture and use it as inspiration to begin a story. For example, if you select a picture of a young girl and a dog, your story might begin "Ana and her dog Loba loved to take walks, because something exciting always happened." One at a time, each child chooses a picture from one of the boxes and uses it to add on to the story. Encourage children to think about what might happen next in the story before they decide which kind of picture to choose (person/animal, place, vehicle). Add other categories of pictures to keep this activity fresh.

- **Toy Stories:** Gather toys and other objects and place them in a box in the center of the circle. With eyes closed, a child selects a toy from the box and starts a story. Offer a framework children can complete until they are comfortable making up their own: "Once upon a time there was a teddy bear and he was owned by _____ who lived _____. One day they went to the _____ and had an adventure. They _____." After volunteering a response to complete the last section ("They _____"), children leave the circle.

Collaborative Nursery Rhyme Inventions

Skills and Concepts
- storytelling
- descriptive language
- sequencing
- patterning

Children are marvelous inventors, and that is as true with words as anything else. Take a few minutes of waiting time to create an innovation on a familiar nursery rhyme together. Once children have created the rhyme, they can chant it as they move to the next activity.

 What to Do

1. Recite a familiar nursery rhyme with children—for example, "Mary, Mary, Quite Contrary."

2. Invite children to take turns changing the characters and events in the rhyme to create a new rhyme. For example, children can change the character in "Mary, Mary, Quite Contrary" to someone in the class with more positive traits! Here's how the new rhyme might go:

   Henry, Henry very happy,
   How does your day go?
   With blocks and snack and jumping jacks,
   And lots of friends all in a row!

Variations

🌀 **Jack and Jill:** Experiment with different nursery rhymes. For example, ask children to add new names to "Jack and Jill." Or, substitute children's names for another Jack and let them "jump over a candlestick" as they transition from one place to another. (See page 58.)

🌀 **Rhymes Our Way:** Take out your favorite nursery rhyme book and invite children to suggest other ways to change the rhymes and make them their own—for example, by changing rhyming pairs of words. Write the new rhymes on chart paper and ask children to illustrate them.

Wee, Wee, Wee All the Way Out

Skills and Concepts

- storytelling
- creative expression
- vocabulary development

One way to make your transitions from group time to activity time smooth and educational is to create variations on the favorite finger play "This Little Piggy." Most children know the rhyme and will delight in creating new ways to "wee, wee, wee all the way out" of the group! Not only will children enjoy brainstorming different ways to move but they will also be building vocabulary and sequencing skills.

What to Do

1. Start by reciting the traditional rhyme "This Little Piggy" together (see right). If possible, write the rhyme on chart paper so children can follow the pattern and sequence of the rhyme.

2. Ask, "If you were a little piggy, how would you move?" Let children take turns suggesting movements and demonstrating them as the class recites the rhyme, replacing the words "wee, wee, wee" with the words that describe each child's movement—for example, "And this little piggy went dancing, dancing, dancing all the way to . . . [fill in the group's destination]. Other forms of movement children might suggest include crawling, hopping, marching, sidestepping, stomping, and tiptoeing.

"This Little Piggy"

This little piggy went to market.
This little piggy stayed at home.
This little piggy had roast beef.
This little piggy had none.
And this little piggy went
"Wee, wee, wee" all the way home.

Variations

Write It! Help children make a visual connection to their words by writing them on chart paper. You can even introduce children to the word *gerund*: action words that end in *-ing*.

Record It! Record children's rhymes. Invite families to listen (or watch) at the end of the day or week. They'll love to see their children acting out innovations on the rhyme.

Let's Pretend

Favorite fairy tales are springboards to moving from one event to another.

Skills and Concepts

- characterization
- expressive language
- creative movement

What to Do

1. Tell a simple, classic story involving animals—for example, "The Three Little Pigs" or "Goldilocks and the Three Bears."

2. Discuss with children how the animals in the story move from place to place. How might they move during different parts of the story? For example, would the pigs move differently once the wolf comes? To help children make connections, you might first discuss different ways people move (*run*, *tiptoe*, *skip*, *crawl*) and reasons people move differently at different times—for example, they might run if they're in a hurry or tiptoe to be quiet.

3. Have children choose a character from the story and then move like that character as they exit circle time. They might also like to add sound effects!

Variations

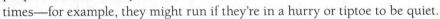

- **Run, Jump, Slide, Glide:** Ask children to brainstorm a list of different sports and games. Discuss different types of movements that each uses—for example, running and jumping for basketball, walking and swinging for golf, and gliding and sliding for ice skating. Have children choose a particular sport and use a movement from that sport as a way to move from one part of the day to another.

- **People on the Move:** Create a chart that depicts different types of jobs that people have. Discuss movements people use in their jobs—for example, a dancer twirls and leaps, a truck driver steers, and a chef chops and stirs. Invite children to pantomime one of those actions as a way to leave circle time and move to the next part of their day.

News Flash

Skills and Concepts

- listening
- sequencing
- vocabulary development
- expressive language

As you well know, young children love (and need) to talk about their lives. The problem is that we often don't have enough time to hear the whole "story" at the class meeting or circle time. Transitions are one of the best times to invite children to share a "news flash." These are brief stories of something children want to share. You can insert News Flash transitions throughout the day and whenever you have an extra bit of time.

What to Do

1. Create a signal to let children know that it is a News Flash time. You might use a blinking flashlight, a hat or visor you put on, or a musical sound.

2. Introduce the concept of News Flash stories by modeling one of your own. Begin by announcing, "News Flash . . . time to listen to the news!" Then share your news, keeping it simple. You will be providing children with a model for the sequence and content of a News Flash story.

3. Invite one child to share his or her news. Then remind children to watch and listen for the next News Flash announcement, at which time another child can take a turn.

Variations

Reporter's Hat: Children may like to make their own news visors to wear when they are the "reporter." Precut crescent tagboard shapes for children to decorate. Tie on elastic cord to create the headband.

Family Share: Record (audio or video) the News Flash stories to share with families. Or, compile News Flash stories in a class newsletter to send home with children to share with their families.

Telephone Connections

Skills and Concepts

- listening
- following directions
- auditory discrimination

Use the traditional telephone game as a fun transition activity. Introduce it by talking about how telephones connect people by sending messages along phone lines. You might ask about how people sent messages and stories years ago before there were telephones and e-mail (methods include drumming, flagging, sending smoke signals, and writing letters). What kinds of stories do children think these messages from long ago told?

What to Do

1. Start the activity by sending a nonverbal message at circle time: Gently squeeze the hand of the child next to you. Have children practice "sending" the squeeze around the circle.

2. Next choose a message to pass around the circle in whispered tones: "Please tell [child's name] that she may leave the circle now. Pass it on." When the message reaches the child named, this child gets up and leaves the circle.

3. Send a new message to excuse the next child. Continue until all children have been named and excused.

Variations

🌀 **Same Meaning, Different Words:** After children are comfortable with and capable of sending the same message around the circle, convey the same meaning but use a slightly different set of words to give the same direction. For example, you might say, "Please invite [child's name] to join the line by the door. Pass this on." or "It is [child's name]'s turn to get up and go!"

🌀 **Add a Ring Tone:** Discuss the types of rings that signal us that someone is calling, such as buzzes, beeps, and songs. Have children demonstrate different sounds and then choose one to add to the game.

Thinking Caps

Use this activity as a mental warm-up exercise before beginning a new project or lesson.

Skills and Concepts

- vocabulary development
- using comparisons and analogies
- creative thinking
- critical thinking

What to Do

1. Have children close their eyes and pretend to put on their thinking caps.

2. Invite them to imagine what their thinking cap looks like. What shape is it? What color is it? How does it feel?

3. Generate some fun, thought-provoking questions that encourage children to compare objects in terms of how they are alike and how they are different. For example:

- How is a dog like a table?
- How are your eyes like a light bulb?
- How is a cup like a house?
- How is a swing like an airplane?
- How is the sun like a frying pan?

4. Encourage use of descriptive details as children discuss their ideas. Then let children create their own questions for the class to answer.

Teaching Tip

Language games enrich vocabulary development and nurture a love of language—building a strong foundation for literacy learning.

Variations

Picture Pairs: Use pictures to generate the questions. Cut out pictures from magazines or old workbooks. Choose any two pictures and ask children how the items are alike and different. Some picture pairs will really stretch children's thinking skills and invite use of detailed language.

Magic Imagination Capes: Have children close their eyes and pretend to put on a magic imagination cape. Ask questions to warm up their thinking skills—for example, "What does your cape look like? What does it feel like? What can you do and where can you go wearing your magic cape? How do you move when you are wearing your magic cape?" Help children expand their vocabulary by choosing questions that require descriptive details in their answers. Invite children to demonstrate how they move when they are wearing their capes and use that mode to move on to the next activity.

Riddle Me!

The fun of riddles is in the guessing. You can use riddles as a "back pocket" activity that you keep at the ready whenever you need children's attention during a transition or before an activity. Just start the riddle and you will have children wondering, thinking, and talking!

Skills and Concepts

- patterning
- sequencing
- vocabulary development
- deductive reasoning
- creative thinking

What to Do

1. Choose a riddle category, such as "animals." Consider a classroom theme or a seasonal connection as a topic for riddles.

2. Make up a riddle for children to solve, using a format that children can follow to make up their own riddles. Following is a sample format for animal riddles. With this format, children fill in the last word in the riddle.

Format:
Line 1: Where I live
Line 2: How I move
Line 3: What I look like
Line 4: I am _____ .

Riddle:
I live in the ocean.
I dive and swim.
I have gills and a fin.
I am _____ [a fish].

Teaching Tip

Maintain a consistent category and pattern with your riddles over a period of a week or so. Children will pick up on the pattern quickly and will have great fun (and success) with both answering and eventually creating riddles. It is important for children to know that the riddles do not have to rhyme. This allows children more opportunities for creative language building.

Variation

- **Rhyming Riddles:** Here's another fun format for animal riddles that will encourage children's rhyming skills:
  There is a [type of animal],
  Whose name is [name].
  I don't know how,
  But he/she can [verb that rhymes with the name]!
  Example: *There is a cat whose name is Kate; I don't know how, but she can skate!* Share all but the last word with children, and then let them fill in the rhyming word to complete the rhyme. Once they've done this a few times, they will be able to use the structure to make up their own riddles.

Knock-Knock

The best part of using knock-knock jokes with young children is that it really doesn't matter if the punch line makes sense—they will laugh anyway! Educationally, knock-knock jokes provide children with experiences that introduce different conventions of language. The unique pattern and sequence makes this joke form easy for children to learn and use. Use knock-knock jokes for a "change-of-pace" mini-game or a time filler while children are waiting.

Skills and Concepts

- patterning
- sequencing
- vocabulary development
- expressive language

 What to Do

1. The basic format is to have children start the joke and have the teacher respond. To begin, have children choose something in the room (such as a window) as the focus of their joke. This word becomes the "Who's there?" response.

2. You can help children find a punch line by asking them to think of a way to describe the "Who's there?" word.

3. When children are ready, let them take turns sharing their jokes. A sample joke session might sound like this:

> Children: Knock, knock.
> Teacher: Who's there?
> Children: Window [or any word].
> Teacher: Window who?
> Children: Window on the wall [or whatever they think is funny!].

Variations

○ **Whose Turn?** Use the knock-knock joke format to excuse two children at a time from the group (or to have children line up two at a time):
Teacher: *Knock, knock.*
Children: *Whose turn?*
Teacher: *Bethany.*
Children: *Bethany and who?*

Teacher: *Bethany and Pat.*
Everyone: *That's who!*
Eventually, children will be able to take turns being the leader.

○ **Knock-Knocks at Home:** Include a few of children's knock-knock jokes in the class newsletter each week. Children will enjoy sharing them with families.

With a Song in My Head . . . and a Dance in My Feet

Skills and Concepts

- expressive language
- sequencing
- listening
- vocabulary development

Children respond well to song variations, perhaps because they are so familiar with the structure and sequence of the song that they can easily create new lyrics that fit the group or the situation. You can use a familiar song to help children transition from one activity to another. They will be building many aspects of language along the way.

 What to Do

1. Sing "Row, Row, Row Your Boat" with the class. Then invite children to hum the tune a few times. You will be giving them an experience with the sound, rhythm, and sequence of the song.

2. Have children choose a movement word, such as *skip*, to replace the word *row* in the song. Then have them suggest a descriptive word for this movement (for the third line of the song). So if their movement word is *skip*, the descriptive word might be *bouncily*.

3. Then use their words to sing a new version of the song:

   Skip, skip, skip our feet,
   Out of circle time.
   Bouncily, bouncily, bouncily, bouncily
   We're off to get in line.

Variations

- **More Ways to Move:** Another day you might ask, "What other movements can we sing and dance to this tune?" Others to consider: *hop*, *step*, *spin*, and *slide*. For example:

  Slide, slide, slide our feet,
  Off to play outside.
  Slippery, slippery, slippery, slippery
  Outside is where we slide.

- **Sing a New Movement Song:** Consider using other movement songs such as "The Wheels on the Bus." Choose special words in the song to have children change—for example, children might change *wheels* to *children* and *bus* to *class* ("The children in the class go . . ."). Children will catch on quickly and offer their own ideas.

Power Pairs

A discussion about pairs reinforces vocabulary for comparisons and serves as a springboard for transitioning a pair of children at a time from one activity to another.

Skills and Concepts

- vocabulary development
- expressive language
- recognizing opposites

 What to Do

1. Lead a discussion about pairs. What makes a pair? (Consider, for example, a pair of shoes or mittens.) Do pairs have to be the same? What else can be a pair? (Consider, for example, two friends or a spoon and fork.) Discuss how items in different pairs go together. What other kinds of things go together?

2. Have one child name something that could be part of a pair—for example, *peanut butter*. Have a second child name something that makes a pair—for example, *jelly*. Encourage children to explain how the items are related. These children then leave the circle together.

3. Repeat until all children have paired up and transitioned to the next activity.

Teaching Tip

As a language extension, discuss words that mean *two*—for example, *pair, partners, twins, duet, double,* and *duo*.

Variations

- **Picture Pairs:** In advance, create or cut out pictures of items that come in pairs. As you prepare to transition from circle time, place the pictures and a pair of big rubber boots in the center of the circle. Invite a child to choose a picture. Have the child name the picture and show it to the group. Invite a second child to find the picture that makes a pair. Children place their pictures in the boots (one picture in each) and exit the group.

- **Opposites:** Generate a list of opposites. Write the words on index cards and give one to each child. Call out a word. Let children name the opposite. Children holding those words leave the circle together. Repeat for all pairs of opposites to excuse all children.

Say It With Puppets

Puppets can be a big help for creating smooth transitions. This is because the puppet becomes an impersonal (and fun) leader, direction giver, and/or rule setter. Interestingly, it is often easier for a child to follow a direction given by a puppet than a person. This might be because children are fascinated with a puppet talking to them! However it works, it's a great tool to keep in your transition-time bag of tricks!

Skills and Concepts

- listening
- following directions
- sequencing
- vocabulary development

 ## What to Do

1. When it's time to transition, bring out a puppet to give children directions. You might use specific puppets for different situations—for example, a "Welcome" puppet, a "Line up'" puppet, and a "Clean up" puppet. Use a different voice for each puppet to give it an identity.

2. Use the puppet to reinforce words that help children follow directions, such as *first*, *next*, and *now*.

Teaching Tip

Finger and hand puppets are readily available but are also easy to make. Glue bits of fabric to make a face on the foot of an old sock or the fingers of a glove. A hollow rubber ball can make a great puppet head. Use marker or fabric scraps to make a face on the ball, then cut a small slit or hole in the bottom to slip your finger in. Children can also help create these puppets. Their involvement makes them more interested in following the directions the puppets give!

Variations

Singing Puppets: Here is a line-up song for the puppet to sing to the tune of "This Is the Way We Wash Our Clothes":
[Child's name] and [new child's name],
Please line up,
Please line up,
Please line up.
[New child's name] and [new child's name],
Please line up.
It's time to go outside.

Personal Puppets: Children might like to make their very own puppets for clean up time. Give each child a disposable plastic glove. (Check for allergies first.) Children can decorate their glove with markers, then put on their puppets when it's time to pick up.

Chat While You Wait!

Skills and Concepts

• expressive language
• taking turns
• listening
• vocabulary development

In any early childhood classroom there is always some waiting time to fill. You might be waiting for a special program or visitor or waiting to go out or go home. Use this magical interlude to inspire and teach good conversation and vocabulary skills.

 What to Do

1. Introduce the topic "Favorites." Discuss what it means to have a favorite something. Share a favorite of your own (such as an author, food, color, or animal).

2. Invite children to suggest favorites of their own—colors, foods, shapes, songs, animals, vegetables, fruits, and so on.

3. Go beyond the "naming" of favorites to a language-building discussion of why something is a favorite.

Teaching Tip

Other great conversation starters include:
• The biggest thing ever . . .
• The smallest thing ever . . .
• The best thing ever . . .
• The funniest thing ever . . .

Variations

Favorites Chart: Add print awareness by recording children's favorites on chart paper. If possible, add simple pictures to illustrate their words and make the list more accessible to young readers. Keep the lists in your meeting or writing area for quick and easy reference.

Theme Favorites: Tie your conversations into a current theme. If you are studying colors, shapes, animals, or the community, invite children to discuss related favorites.

A Symphony of Words

Have you ever heard the cacophony of night sounds in nature? They are a wonderful mixture of unrelated sounds, both high-pitched and low, that together create a symphony of sound. You can create a similar sound in your classroom using vocabulary words. This is a great way to take a "silly break" when things are getting too tense in the classroom.

Skills and Concepts

* vocabulary development
* listening
* expressive language

 What to Do

1. Choose a category of words. You can select a category that corresponds with a current curriculum theme. For example, if you're studying healthy foods, you might choose Vegetables as a category.

2. Brainstorm with children different vegetables, and list them on chart paper.

3. Divide the class into three groups. Invite each group to choose a word from the list. Have children in each group practice saying their word together.

4. Assign each group a way to say their word—for example, in a deep voice, in a squeaky high voice, and in a whisper. Give children time to practice saying their word in this voice.

5. Use a pencil or dowel as a conductor's baton and strike up the symphony. Tell children to watch your baton and start saying their word (in their special voices) when you make a downbeat. You can raise your baton when you went them to say the word louder and then end the symphony by lowering your baton to make the sound get quieter and quieter, until the symphony is silent.

Variations

🔹 **Vegetables We Love and Hate:** You might want to start with vegetables children love the first time you play the game and do the ones they hate the next time around. (Group children by vegetables they agree on.) Encourage children to use "yucky" sounds and make funny faces when they say the words. Don't laugh!

🔹 **Animal Sounds:** Substitute animal sounds for an especially silly experience. Let children select a category of animals, such as farm animals or forest animals. Have each group choose an animal and practice the sound that animal makes. Bring groups together for a symphony of animal sounds.

Red Light, Green Light

Being able to transition well requires understanding initiation and then cessation of an activity. With practice, children learn to recognize the words that signal beginnings and endings—especially when they use their entire bodies to act out the concepts.

Skills and Concepts

• listening
• following directions
• synonyms

What to Do

1. Have children lie on the floor, keeping their torsos still. Once everyone is settled, call out, "Red light, green light, one, two, three. Start!" At this signal, children slowly lift their arms and legs, waving them in the air back and forth and up and down. After a moment or so call out, "Red light, green light, one, two, three. Stop!" All movement must stop and children need to lie still again.

2. Repeat this several times, substituting words that have the same meaning as *start* and *stop*—for example, *begin, go, commence, end, halt, finish, conclude, cease.*

Variations

● **Stand and Scatter:** Children stand scattered in an open area. Using the same "red light, green light" directions, have children practice starting and stopping. At first, begin with slow movements, increasing the tempo to include faster movements and quicker physical transitions.

● **Red Means *Stop*:** Use red and green signs to signal when students start and stop moving. Include the corresponding color word on each sign to build word recognition. As an extension, explore color and shape symbols and what they mean.

How Many Words for a Group?

Young children love to learn new and interesting words (even big ones) when the words are presented in the context of a fun activity. Transition time is just right for introducing new words. This activity teaches names for groups of animals, and invites children to practice the meaning of each word as they move on to their next activity.

Skills and Concepts

- vocabulary development
- expressive language
- creative movement
- cooperating

 What to Do

1. Introduce words that name groups of animals, such as a *gaggle* of geese, *pride* of lions, and *school* of fish. Write the words on a chart. Add pictures if possible to help children make connections between the spoken and written words.

2. Use these words as a fun way to excuse children from the group with different movements. One group can move like a school of fish, another like a gaggle of geese, and so on. Best of all, children have to use teamwork to be able to move as a group instead of the traditional way of transitioning one or two at a time.

Teaching Tip

Children will have fun adding new words and movements to their repertoire. Review the list periodically to see if children remember the word for a group of hens (*brood*) or puppies (*litter*).

Variations

🌀 **Big Book of Groups:** Invite children to create drawings to illustrate the animal groups. Put these together in a class "Big Book of Groups."

🌀 **New Names:** Take it one step further by inviting children to make up their own funny names for groups of things. For example, ask, "What would be the word for a group of crayons?"

Focus . . . Focus . . . Freeze!

In order to develop strong descriptive language skills, children need to be able to observe and focus their attention on details. In this activity, children will be learning to slow down enough to be observant and will be encouraged to extend their use of descriptive language.

Skills and Concepts

- following directions
- observing
- descriptive language
- vocabulary development
- taking turns

What to Do

1. Share a pair of binoculars to demonstrate how they work. Have children use their hands to encircle their eyes as if they were using binoculars. Ask: "How does that change what you see? Why do things look different?"

2. Have children look all around through their "binoculars" (hands) as you chant the following:

   Look up and down and toward the ground.
   Look up and down and all around.
   Focus . . . focus . . . freeze!

3. Children stop and freeze, looking at one thing. Ask: " What do you see?" Children in turn answer by naming what they are focused on: "I see. . . ."

4. Repeat the chant and again ask children to describe what they see. This time have children name and describe what they see, adding one word—for example, "I see a red crayon" or "I see an untied boot." Try this again with two or more describing words.

Teaching Tip

Children can make simple binoculars out of cardboard tubes and yarn and use them for this activity. Help them tape two tubes side by side and tie on yarn.

Variations

- **On and Under:** Change the parameters. Ask, "What do you see that is *on* something?" ("I see blocks on the rug.") Or "What do you see that is *under* something?" ("I see a hamster under the shelves!") "What do you see that is *next to* something?" ("I see Rose next to the easel.")

- **Flashlight Focus:** Shine a flashlight in a darkened room to focus children's attention on an object. Together the class can offer descriptions of what is contained in the beam of light.

Passports, Please!

With this activity, "passports" help children learn to travel from one center to another.

Skills and Concepts

• vocabulary development
• writing
• taking turns

What to Do

1. In preparation, have children put blank paper together to make small booklets that look like passports. They can write their names and decorate the covers. Set up a passport "station" at each center—for example, provide date stamps (to teach names for days of the week and months) and stickers.

2. Discuss how people use passports to travel between countries. If possible, share a passport or pictures of a passport to provide a visual.

3. As children go to a center, have them stamp one another's passports to show they have visited that area of the classroom.

4. Have children repeat this for each center they visit.

Variations

○ **Travel Center:** Set up a center that is an airport, train station, or travel agency. Include maps, posters, travel brochures, flags, and a globe. Provide writing and art materials so children can create their own tickets, passports, forms, and brochures.

○ **Travel Talk:** Introduce words that relate to travel, such as *arrival* and *departure*. Invite children to name words that mean the same thing (such as *come* and *go*).

Quickly, Quietly

Skills and Concepts

- descriptive vocabulary
- creative movement
- following directions

It is always fun to use animal movements to excuse children from a group activity, but you can take this teachable moment one step further by adding a language and vocabulary component.

What to Do

1. Brainstorm descriptive words for ways animals move—for example, *quickly, quietly, sneakily,* and *speedily.* You might start by listing animals children know and then discussing how they move.

2. Invite children to choose one of the animals and exit from the group as that animal would.

Teaching Tip

Throughout the year, repeat this activity with new words and animals. Collect the words on chart paper and use for writing prompts.

Variations

- **Quick as a Cricket:** Inspire children's interest in descriptive language by sharing *Quick as a Cricket* by Audrey Wood (Scholastic, 1994). Follow up by inviting children to suggest other phrases that describe animals in some way, such as "slow as a turtle." Copy each phrase onto a large sheet of paper and let children illustrate, then compile to make a class Big Book.

- **Biggest, Smallest, Fastest:** Explore superlatives (such as *biggest, smallest, fastest*). Ask: "Can you imagine the biggest animal? How would it move? How would the smallest animal move?" Share *Biggest, Strongest, Fastest* by Steve Jenkins (Ticknor & Fields, 1995) for inspiration. From a tiny flea to the mammoth blue whale, this book shares records that animals set for being the biggest, smallest, fastest, slowest, and everything in between.

You're Hot . . . You're Cold . . . You're HOT!

There is something so powerful about the traditional guessing game "Hot and Cold." In a very simple and fun way it introduces children to vocabulary and invites them to use listening as a means for developing directionality.

Skills and Concepts

- vocabulary development
- recognizing opposites
- listening
- spatial relationships

What to Do

1. Begin by playing a few games of the traditional game "Hot and Cold." Hide something in the room while one child is not looking and ask the others to guide the child closer and closer to the hidden object by using the words *hot* (getting closer) and *cold* (going farther away). When the child gets very close, the other children can say things like "really hot" and "really, really hot!"

2. Then try a variation on the game to transition a group to a particular learning center. The fun is not only in the listening but also in finding the destination! Have a group of four or five children cover their eyes while you point out to the rest of the class which learning center the group is going to.

3. Have children open their eyes and start moving together toward a center. The class directs them by saying "hot" or "cold" until they get there!

Variations

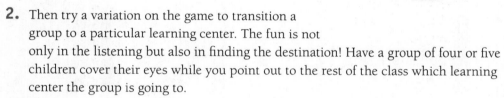

Hidden Treasure: Sometimes it's fun to play "Hot and Cold" to find a treasure. When you have a few extra minutes to fill, hide a few stickers (or other small "treasures") for children to find (one group at a time). Use the "hot" and "cold" directions to guide them to the hiding place.

Left, Right, Forward, Back: Guide children to their destination by using directional words. Let children practice using the words themselves by hiding something for you to find.

Jump-Rope Rants and Chants

Skills and Concepts

- expressive language
- rhyming
- listening
- taking turns

The rhythm and rhyme of jump-rope chants make them a very accessible poetic form for young children to learn. Use them as children exit circle time, return to the class, or simply as a fun game.

 What to Do

1. Chant the following rhymes with children a few times so they become familiar with the words and the rhythm:

   I like toast, I like tea,
   I'd like [name of next person in the circle or line] to leave with me!

   I like the ocean, I like the sea,
   I'd like [next child's name] to leave with me!

2. Let children take turns choosing and chanting one of the rhymes, and inviting the person next to them to join them as they leave the circle in pairs.

I like toast, I like tea, I'd like BESS to leave with me.

Variation

Sailors at Sea: Invite children to act out a transition rhyme (right) as they chant it, placing their hand above their brow as if searching at sea. After completing the rhyme by naming two children, have those children exit the circle. Repeat the rhyme as needed to excuse all children.

A sailor went to sea, sea, sea.
To see what (s)he could see, see, see.
But all that (s)he could see, see, see
Was [names of two children who then leave the circle] leaving the circle.

Birthday Rhymes

Children need to know the name of their birthday month. These chants can help to reinforce their birthdays and the names for the months of the year.

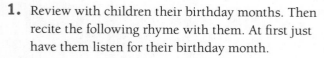

What to Do

1. Review with children their birthday months. Then recite the following rhyme with them. At first just have them listen for their birthday month.

> Apples, peaches, pears, and plums.
> Tell me when your birthday comes.
> January, February, March, April . . . [etc.].

2. Repeat the rhyme, this time having children leave the circle when their birthday month is named.

Variations

● **Birthday Bluebirds:** Here is another birthday chant to try.

> Two little bluebirds sittin' on the wall.
> One named Peter, one named Paul. [Children wave their arms like birds.]
> Fly away, Peter; fly away, Paul.
> Don't fly away until your birthday is called.
> January, February, March . . . [etc.].

As children hear their birthday month called, they flap their arms to fly away from the circle. As the last of the children leave, chant:

> Now fly away, fly away, fly away all.

Jack, Jump!

One of the best ways for children to internalize poetry is to act it out. Familiar nursery rhymes or finger plays are just right for these active transitions from circle time to another activity.

Skills and Concepts

- patterning
- sequencing
- rhyming
- following directions

 ## What to Do

1. With children, chant the nursery rhyme "Jack Be Nimble":

   Jack be nimble,

   Jack be quick,

   Jack jumped over the candlestick.

2. Repeat the rhyme to transition children from circle time, substituting each child's name in place of *Jack*. Children can jump over a small, unlit candle in the center of the circle as they hear their name and proceed to leave.

Variation

Frog Hop: Try a new version of the poem in which Jack is a frog.

Frog be agile, frog be fast.

Frog hopped over the lily pad.

Repeat the rhyme to transition children from circle time, substituting each child's name in place of *Frog*. Children can hop over a rug square representing a lily pad or a picture of a lily pad placed in the middle of the circle, and then continue hopping right out of the meeting area!

In and Out the Windows

Skills and Concepts

- rhyming
- creative movement
- sequencing
- following directions

When is a poem more than a poem? When it's a song! As you well know, songs are a very accessible form of poetry for young children because the repetition, rhythm, and rhyme help children hear and remember the poetic pattern. Use the classic movement song "Go In and Out the Window" as a fun way to transition children off the playground and into the classroom.

What to Do

1. Have children form a giant "building" by standing in a circle with arms stretched out at shoulder height. (Guide children to space themselves out enough to make room for their arms.) They then join hands with their neighbor to create "windows" in the building.

2. As you and the children sing a variation on the song "Go In and Out the Window" (see right), one child goes around the circle weaving in and out the windows (the spaces between children).

3. While the class sings the second verse, the child chooses a partner and the two proceed to get in line.

4. Repeat the first and second verses until all children are in line. Sing the last verse together as children return to their classroom.

"Go In and Out the Window"

Go in and out the windows.
Go in and out the windows.
Go in and out the windows,
As we have done before.

Stop and choose a partner.
Stop and choose a partner.
Stop and choose a partner,
As we have done before.

Now follow to the classroom.
Now follow to the classroom.
Now follow to the classroom,
As we have done before.

Variations

 Make a Train: Instead of having children line up in pairs, have them make a giant train as each pair joins the line. Then send the class off with the third verse!

Sing a New Verse: Use the song as a model for creating new verses. Instead of going in and out the windows, for example, children might go "round and round the apple tree."

The Shape of Poetry

Creating a shape poem is an excellent transition activity to fill waiting time or to calm and center the group. Shape poems are also one of the easiest ways to introduce young children to creating their own poems, because all they really have to do is brainstorm a list of words!

Skills and Concepts

- expressive language
- patterning
- sequencing
- vocabulary development

 What to Do

Teaching Tip

Shape poems are an excellent precursor for more detailed poem patterns such as lanterne and cinquain. (See pages 59–60.)

1. Share a shape poem with children. Write the poem on chart paper and read it aloud with children. Guide children to notice that the words are in the shape of the poem's subject. Here's a sample shape poem:

2. Invite children to suggest a good shape for a poem about snow (a snowflake or snowman) or rain (a raindrop or an umbrella).

3. Create a shape poem together. Draw an outline of a snowflake on chart paper. Invite children to brainstorm words that describe snow—for example, *cold*, *white*, *slippery*, *fluffy*, and *flakes*. Write their words on the lines that form the shape of the snowflake. At the end of the activity read the poem with children. You can start the poem by saying, "Snow is. . . ."

Variations

Poetry Charts: You can use this form of poetry to support classroom themes. Try to create a shape poem for each unit of study. Record the poems on chart paper and display on an easel or in a Big Book in the writing center. Children can use the poems as inspiration for creating their own shape poems.

Math Connections: Invite children to write shape poems to tell what they know about shapes, such as a triangle, square, or circle.

Take a Lanterne Break

Skills and Concepts

- expressive language
- patterning
- sequencing
- vocabulary development

Sometimes the best way to settle children and regain their attention is to make a dramatic shift in activity and engage them in a mini-lesson. The surprise transition will get children's attention and the content of the activity will make it fun!

 What to Do

1. Introduce children to lanterne poems, in which five lines form the shape of a Japanese lantern. Share an example, and let children recite it with you and clap out the syllables in each line.

> The
> frog is
> happily
> jumping on the
> log.

2. Revisit each line and count the syllables together (in order, 1, 2, 3, 4, and 1). Provide children with a simple line-by-line pattern to follow:

> 1 syllable
> 2 syllables
> 3 syllables
> 4 syllables
> 1 syllable

3. Invite children to use the pattern to create a new lanterne poem. You might suggest they choose another animal. Have them offer ideas for what the animal might be doing. List children's ideas on chart paper. Then invite them to see which words fit the pattern. (You might circle those that do to eliminate confusion.) Children might suggest:

> The
> fat fox
> is running
> around the red
> barn.

Teaching Tip

Remember that writing "for" children is an important precursor to writing "with" them. Don't worry if children are not ready to create a poem. Just enjoy modeling the process.

Variation

 Favorite Lanternes: Children love discussing favorites—favorite foods, colors, games, books, and so on. Invite children to use this topic as a source for new poems. Collate each child's poems to make a personal collection of poetry to share with families.

Cinquain Me!

Once children have had some practice with shape and lanterne poems, they are ready to try cinquain poetry. You can use the pattern of this five-line poem to create personal poems for each child.

Skills and Concepts

• expressive language
• patterning
• sequencing
• vocabulary development
• parts of speech

What to Do

1. Share a cinquain with children, for example:

       Dawn
       Shy, quiet
       Reading, walking, drawing
       Like a tiny mouse
       Dawn

2. Let children write cinquains to tell something about themselves. The word-count format may be easiest for young children to follow.

       Line 1: your name
       Line 2: two words that describe you
       Line 3: three actions or things you like to do
       Line 4: a sentence about yourself
       Line 5: your name

What Is a Cinquain?

A cinquain is a poem written in five lines organized by word count or by syllables.

By word count:

Line 1: one word, a noun
Line 2: two adjectives
Line 3: three action words (or gerunds)
Line 4: a statement of four words (or four adjectives)
Line 5: a synonym for the first word (or the repetition of the first word)

By syllable count:

Line 1: 2 syllables
Line 2: 4 syllables
Line 3: 6 syllables
Line 4: 8 syllables
Line 5: 2 syllables

Variations

🔹 **Weekly Poem:** Feature one child per week in a poem. By the end of the year you will have a highly personalized collection of poetry.

🔹 **Poetic Photo Album:** Take photos of children to illustrate their poems. Put their pages together to create a class album. Make copies for children and families at the end of the year.

Math Transitions

Transition time is an excellent time to introduce, revisit, and reinforce all the wonderful math skills you teach throughout the day. Math transitions provide children with a "short and sweet" math exploration that can capture their attention, engage their thinking, and encourage them to use the language of math as they verbalize their experiences.

Math transition activities support children in developing skills in the content areas of number and operations, geometry, data analysis, and algebra, while at the same time promoting the areas of problem solving, reasoning, communication, and making connections. (For a comprehensive list of math and other skills, see pages 7–8.) Often an activity in a particular math topic will integrate skills and concepts from other areas. These are highlighted in the Skills and Concepts section for each activity.

Explore using the activities for different types of transition times, including getting from one place to another, calming and centering, using up excess energy, and filling wait time. You will find that the more you revisit a particular activity, the more children get out of the experience. Each time you repeat an activity, children's prior knowledge will guide the activity to new and deeper levels of understanding. By building on children's knowledge base and adjusting the approach or content, these math transition activities become new every time you use them!

Section Organizer

The transition activities in this section are grouped by the following topics:

Counting and Estimating (pages 62–72)

Sorting and Classifying (pages 73–80)

Sequencing, Patterning, and Seriating (pages 81–90)

Adding and Subtracting (pages 91–99)

Measuring (pages 100–105)

Graphing (pages 106–111)

It's About Time!

Sometimes the most difficult part about gathering children is getting them to stop what they are doing in a timely fashion. So why not use time as part of the game and introduce some math concepts at the same time?

Skills and Concepts

- counting
- number recognition
- time
- ordinal numbers

What to Do

1. Set a windup timer for two minutes; announce that when the timer goes off, it is time to come to group.

2. When children arrive at the circle, pass out numeral cards in order of their arrival (1, 2, 3, and so on).

3. When everyone has arrived and has a card, have children read the numerals on their cards, beginning with "1."

4. As children count, have them place their cards in order on the floor or on a whiteboard tray. This will enable children to see a number line that represents their arrival to the group.

5. Read the number line together.

Teaching Tip

This transition technique is highly motivating, since, as you well know, most young children want to be first at everything!

Variations

🌀 **To and From:** Return the cards to children and use them to excuse children in numeric order from circle time. (Children may have different cards at this time than they had when they arrived.)

🌀 **How Many Minutes?** Use the timer to find out how long it takes everyone to get to group. Keep a record of the times over a period of time, such as a week, to see if children can improve their time. Invite children to estimate how long it will take them.

🌀 **Ordinal Numbers:** Use the numeral cards to introduce ordinal numbers. (You might add the words for ordinal numbers to the cards to reinforce the connection.) Read the cards beginning with *first*.

Counting Off Attendance

Skills and Concepts

- counting
- small-motor development
- number recognition

The process of counting off in a row can be difficult for children, but if you make it tangible and fun they learn very quickly! Use this activity to make attendance part of a transition time instead of using valuable circle-time minutes for this morning routine.

 What to Do

1. Provide large beads and a shoelace and have children string one bead as they arrive at morning meeting or circle time.

2. After stringing their bead, have children stand in the circle and remain standing until everyone is there and the class is ready to count off. Remember, you need to stand, too!

3. Model saying "one" and then sitting down. Signal the child next to you to say "two" and join you in sitting down.

4. Continue around the circle in this way, having children sit down as they say their number. The process of sitting after saying their number adds a kinesthetic connection to the counting experience.

5. Together, count the beads on the shoelace. How many beads? How many children?

Teaching Tip

As an alternative to stringing beads, children can also string dried pasta tubes or they can tie knots in a rope to signal their arrival to morning meeting.

Variations

Counting With Cards: Eventually you can give children numeral and/or number word cards so they can see the number as they say it.

Add Estimation: Add the skill of estimating. Invite children to estimate how many children are present before counting off. Record their estimate, and compare the actual number. As children repeat this over a period of a week or a month, their estimates will become increasingly more accurate.

Count Down to Blastoff!

When children are restless, distracted, or just a bit wild, this NASA-inspired countdown will get their attention in no time. This transition activity also reinforces the difficult skill of counting backwards.

Skills and Concepts

- counting (backwards)
- sequencing
- number recognition

What to Do

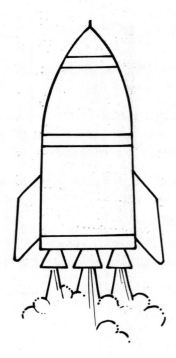

1. Begin by announcing, in an official NASA voice, "Blastoff to circle time [or any other class activity] is T-minus ten seconds."

2. Count down from ten: "Ten . . . nine . . . eight . . ." and so on, ending with "Blastoff!" Children usually chime in quickly and enjoy making an explosive motion when they say "Blastoff!" Then quickly engage them in your chosen activity while you have their full attention.

Variations

- **Number Pointer:** Post a number line (0–10) and invite a volunteer to use a pointer to point to each number in turn (10, 9, 8, and so on) as you're counting down.

- **Add Movement:** Let children choose a motion to add to their countdown, such as foot stomping or hand clapping.

Counting-Off Cooperation Rhyme

Use a counting rhyme to gather and motivate classroom helpers.

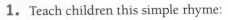 **What to Do**

1. Teach children this simple rhyme:

   It takes many helpers
   To get all our big jobs done.
   More than two or three
   Makes the classroom fun.
   The more we help each other
   The happier we will be.
   How many does it take to [name job]?
   Let's count off and see:
   1 . . . 2 . . . 3 . . . [etc.].

2. Use the rhyme to count off the appropriate number of helpers for each job. For example, you might count off three to pick up blocks and four to tidy the dramatic play area.

Variations

● **Wave a Wand:** A magic wand adds a special effect to this activity. To make a wand, top a dowel with a sparkling star and tie on a few curly ribbons. Children will enjoy taking over this job, using the wand to help with the count-off.

● **Pick a Job:** Write names for jobs on large index cards and draw a representative picture that depicts the number of students for that task. When it's time to clean up, let children take turns selecting a card at random and leading the count-off for this job.

It's Dicey

Children are fascinated with dice. An oversized die is a wonderful way to introduce numeration as children move from one activity to another.

Skills and Concepts

- counting
- recognizing quantities
- numeration

What to Do

1. Make a giant die out of a square box or container (see right). Draw from one to six dots (or use sticky dots) on each side to mimic the look of a regular die.

2. Invite children to take turns rolling the die. Have them announce the number they roll, and then invite that many children to join them as they move on to the next activity. For example, a child who rolls 3 takes three more children along (for a total of four children).

Variations

How Many More? Have children take turns rolling and then using the number they roll to tell how many more children will join them to equal the number shown on the die. In this case, a child who rolls 3 will take along two more children.

Roll Two: Have children roll a pair of dice to take from 1 to 12 children with them. Or, have them roll to see how many steps they can take to go on to the next activity. They keep rolling until they arrive! (For this variation, you may want to provide pairs of children with dice and have them roll and transition together.)

Take a Number

Just like at the deli counter, children can take a number and practice the important transition skill of taking turns.

Skills and Concepts

- counting
- taking turns
- number recognition
- sequencing

What to Do

1. Decorate a small box with numerals. Fill it with number cards, number blocks, or number tiles.

2. As children transition to circle time, ask them if they would like a turn to share something (such as something that happened, a book they enjoyed, or special news). If they would, have them reach inside the box and take a number.

3. Place a simple number line in the area so children can match their number. This will give them a sense of when their turn will happen. Remember, there may not be enough time for all children in the class to take a turn each day. Limit the number of numeral cards you let children take to match the time available. Be sure to record the names of children who share each day so that everyone gets a turn (if they want) during the week.

Variations

- **Center-Time Turns:** Use this take-a-number approach to give children time at a popular center, such as the block corner or dramatic play area.

- **Playground Practice:** Let children take a number for taking turns on popular playground equipment. Or use the technique to rotate children into a favorite game, such as hopscotch.

Number Line Buddies

Skills and Concepts

- counting
- matching
- one-to-one correspondence

An important part of learning to count is the process of matching sets of objects in numeric order. That is why two number lines are better than one! This is an excellent, quiet transition activity to use when a small group of children need a calm, purposeful activity.

 What to Do

1. Bring two sets of math counters (such as teddy bears and frogs) and two matching sets of numeral cards to your circle time area. Divide the group in half and have children sit back to back. (You will want to have the same number of children in each group so everyone has a partner.)

2. Give the first child in one group the numeral card for 1 and have that child take one math counter. Repeat in order for each child in this group, with all children counting out the same type of counter. Have children place their numeral card and counters on the floor in front of them.

3. Repeat step 2 with the second group of children and the other set of numeral cards and counters.

4. Have children turn around to meet their "back-to-back" partner—the child who has the same numeral card and same number of counters.

5. Once children have shared and compared with their partners, have them stand (with their cards and counters) to create two parallel number lines. Children can read aloud their numbers in pairs, beginning with "1." Then off they go!

Variations

- **Mixed-Up Buddies:** For a more challenging version, let children in each group randomly choose a numeral card. When children in each group have their numeral card and counters, have them find their partners, then arrange themselves by pairs in numeric order to form two number lines.

- **Backwards Buddies:** Children can arrange themselves in order beginning with the highest number first and counting backwards.

Give Me Three!

An important part of children's mathematical development is understanding that numbers can tell how many of something. In this fun transition game, children demonstrate this understanding of number as they move from one activity to another.

Skills and Concepts

- counting
- numeration
- large-motor development
- number recognition

What to Do

1. When it is time to transition to a new activity, pull out a set of numeral cards (1–5 or 1–10).

2. Choose a movement for children to make, such as clapping hands. Invite a child to select a card and tell what number is on the card. Invite the child to show that number in claps. You might say, for example, "What number is on your card? Can you show me that number in claps? Great; off you go to snack!"

3. Have the other children take turns selecting a number card, telling what number is on their card, and performing the movement that number of times as they transition to the next activity.

Teaching Tip

Try this activity with a variety of hand, finger, and foot movements. Remember to get silly, too. Add some wiggles, spins, and winks!

Variations

 Chant Along: Encourage the other children to chime in on the counting as each child takes a card and performs the movement.

 Pick a Movement, Any Movement: Eventually children can draw a numeral card and choose their own movement to perform as they count and transition to the next activity.

A Classroom Object Number Line

Number line activities are a great way to help children make the transition from rote counting (reciting numbers from memory) to rational counting (counting actual objects using one-to-one correspondence). In this activity, children gather items from around the classroom and place them in the correct quantity on a craft-paper number line.

 What to Do

1. Divide a long strip of craft paper into ten equal, connected boxes. Number the squares from 1 to 10 to create a number line. Place a corresponding number of sticky dots (or draw them) in each box.

2. Send children on a hunt in the classroom to pick up small items such as blocks, crayons, counters, and books. Invite children to sort the items into piles to see how many they found of each object.

3. Have children choose items to place in the number line. Ask: "How many objects should we put in square number one? Which objects should be placed in square number two? How many?" Children may have to go looking for more objects to fill some of the squares. This will encourage them to use more one-to-one correspondence skills.

4. Have children read the number line when it is finished. They can name the objects as they count from one to ten ("one ruler… two buttons… three crayons…" and so on).

Variations

🔘 **Number Line Performance:** Assign each box on the number line to a small group of children (two to three children per group). Read the number line, letting children in each group add their part in order, using whatever voices (or expression) they choose.

🔘 **Sidewalk Number Line:** On a beautiful day, take the activity outside and make a sidewalk number line using chalk to mark the boxes. Children might look for items in nature to fill in the boxes.

Count and Sing the Number Line

Skills and Concepts

- counting
- number recognition
- one-to-one correspondence

Use the old favorite song "Johnny Works With One Hammer" as the basis for a counting transition activity.

 ## What to Do

1. Set up a classroom number line on a low table or on the floor, drawing ten connected boxes on craft paper and labeling them in order from 1–10.

2. Choose a set of objects for children to arrange on the number line, such as blocks. Invite children to investigate the number line during free time, counting out the corresponding number of objects to go in each box. They can change the objects (for example, replacing a red block in box 1 with a blue block) as often as they like, but they need to maintain the correct number of items in each box.

3. When it's time to transition, have children sing a variation on "Johnny Works With One Hammer" as they take turns removing objects in order from the number line, counting as they do so. Here's how the variation on the song works, using blocks as an example:

   Jane works with one block
   One block, one block.
   [Child's name] works with one block,
   Then William works with two.
   William works with two blocks
   Two blocks, two blocks.
   William works with two blocks
   Then Tenzin works with three.
   [Continue, substituting a new child's name for each new number.]

   Teaching Tip

   For a more durable number line, laminate the paper after drawing and labeling the boxes. Or place ten shoe-box lids side by side (use alligator clips to attach one to another, if desired) and label them 1–10.

4. When you reach 10, change the last line to "And then we go to [insert your destination, such as "lunch."] Repeat this activity on another day to include any children who didn't have a chance to work with the number line this time. Or, repeat the song, having children place the objects back in the boxes this time.

Variations

- **Collection Sort:** Let children use the number line to sort and organize their collections.

- **Cleanup Number Line:** Let children place items in the boxes that need to be put away.

Estimating Partners

Estimating and counting is a lot more fun with a partner!

Skills and Concepts

- observing
- estimating
- counting
- number recognition

What to Do

1. Find an interesting box, plastic vase, or other container. Have on hand enough small objects (such as beads, cubes, or buttons) to fill it.

2. At transition time, display the container and objects for children to observe and investigate. Have children team up with partners and make estimates of how many objects will fill the container. (Don't worry about accuracy of estimates. It is the process that is important at this stage.) Encourage partners to quietly talk with each other about their estimates before agreeing on one.

3. When children are ready, record their names and estimates on chart paper and send them off to the next activity.

4. Later in the day at another transition time (or group time), let children work together to fill the container as they count. Which team's estimate was most accurate?

Variations

Estimating Steps: Have partners guess how many steps it will take for them to walk from circle to the door, or from the snack table to circle. Record estimates, and then count to find out.

How Many? Present a clear container already full of counters, buttons, or other small objects. Let children talk with their partners about how many objects are in the container. Record estimates and then at the next transition time count together to find out.

It's All the Same to Me!

The first step in understanding sorting and classifying is to explore the concept of matching things that are the same. This can also be a good time to introduce the concept of *equal*. Try this simple attribute game as a quiet transition activity.

Skills and Concepts

- matching
- comparing
- sorting
- one-to-one correspondence
- equal to (concept of)

What to Do

1. In advance, gather a set of math counters, such as teddy bears or cubes, or household items, such as buttons or keys. Place the counters in the center of the group and ask children what they notice about them. Children may first describe the objects and how they are used before they notice that they are all the same.

2. Provide sheets of construction paper to place the collection on. (Have extra sheets of construction paper on hand for the next phase of the game.)

3. Now display a combination of additional objects, providing the same number of each type. Ask: "Can we find other sets of objects that are the same?" Encourage children to work together to sort the items onto separate sheets of paper.

4. Once the sorting is complete, guide children in investigating their collections. "What do you notice about your collections? How are they the same? How many objects do you think are in each pile? Let's count and see!" As children count, write the totals for each set on the corresponding paper. After all the counting is complete, ask children what they notice about the amounts. (*They are the same, or equal.*)

5. Further explore the concept of equal by asking, "How can we be sure they are equal?" Have children line up the objects in each collection across from each other to create lines of one-to-one correspondence. Children will quickly see that one teddy bear counter is equal to one button, which is equal to one key!

Teaching Tip

It is best to introduce this activity with objects that are clearly the same by a very recognizable attribute such as color or shape—for example, red teddy bear counters or silver-colored keys.

Variations

- **Same as Me:** Reinforce the concept of same by asking children to look around the room for something that is the same as them in some way—for example, someone who is the same size as they are, or something that is the same color as what they are wearing.

- **Partner Math:** Reinforce the concept of equal whenever you are taking attendance or lining up. Count with children how many boys and how many girls there are that day. Ask: "Is there an equal number?" Have children take a partner to line up. Ask: "Do we have an equal number of friends today so that everyone has a partner?"

Cleanup Time Sort

Cleanup time can be one of the biggest transition problems if children are not clear about the task at hand. You can help organize children and develop math skills by turning cleanup into a sorting activity!

Skills and Concepts

- sorting
- classifying
- problem solving

 What to Do

1. The first step to successful cleanup is to know where things go. Bring a number of classroom materials to circle time and have children sort them according to where they need to be put away. For example, children might place items that belong in the block center in one pile and those that belong in the art center in another.

2. Invite children to place in sorting piles other materials that need to be put away. Then let everyone take something to put away as they move on to the next activity.

Teaching Tip

Cut out pictures from school catalogs to create labels that correspond to different learning centers (where children might put things away at cleanup time). Children can sort the items into groups according to these labels.

Variations

Sing a Cleanup Song: Add a cleanup song to the tune of "Row, Row, Row Your Boat":

> We put toys away
> It won't take all day
> Put away, put away, put away, put away
> We put toys away.
>
> The cars go with the blocks
> The cars go with the blocks
> Put away, put away, put away, put away
> The cars go with the blocks.

Adding Attributes: To add more math to the start of the activity, have children first sort the classroom items in several different ways—for example, they might choose to sort by color, shape, or size. It is important for children to see that materials can be sorted in many different ways.

The "Sort of . . ." Game

Skills and Concepts

• observing
• comparing
• describing
• sorting

Here is a fun circle game that will get children thinking about how colors relate to one another. The challenge is that no two colors in this game will actually match, so children will have to observe subtle differences of shades and hues. Use this activity any time you need a change of pace, or when you have a few minutes to fill.

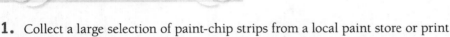

What to Do

1. Collect a large selection of paint-chip strips from a local paint store or print them from the Internet. (Cut apart strips that have more than one color, so children can manipulate each color separately.)

2. Place the paint chips in the center of the circle. (You can fan them out or place them randomly.)

3. Randomly choose one of the paint chips. Show it to children and invite a volunteer to find another chip that is "sort of" similar. Encourage the child to explain how the chips are alike. For example, the chips might be a similar shade or the same hue (light or dark).

4. The child passes the two paint chips to the next child, who chooses a new chip that sort of matches and explains how. This continues until everyone who wants a chance has had one. At the end, display the collection in a row so that children can discuss what they notice about the colors.

Variations

Creating Colors: Extend the activity into arts and crafts time by providing tempera paint for children to replicate the colors they sorted in the game.

Walk and Match: Take the paint chips for a walk! Invite children to use them to observe shades and hues of color in the world around them. Where do they notice the colors on the paint chips? Can they find something that matches a paint chip exactly or "sort of" matches it?

Sort Yourself!

Lining up can be loads of fun when children sort themselves according to colors they are wearing!

Skills and Concepts

• observing
• comparing
• sorting
• classifying

What to Do

1. When it is time to go to lunch, recess, or another place, choose a color by which children can first sort themselves.

2. Call out the color. Have children wearing that color find a partner who is wearing the same color, and then stand together in line. (Explain that the color doesn't have to be exact but close.)

3. Choose another color and repeat. Once everyone is standing in line with a partner, children can march off to their destination.

Variations

○ **Add a Song:** Use this song to help with sorting by color.

"Sort Yourself"
(sing to the tune of "The Farmer in the Dell")

If you are wearing red
You can stand right up.
Now go and find a partner
And please line up.

○ **Sort by Favorites:** Children love to share favorites. When it's time to line up, choose a category. Call out a favorite within that category—for example, "If your favorite outdoor game is kick ball, stand and find a partner. Then line up." Continue naming other choices until all children are in line.

Let's Be Pirates

Take sorting and classifying out to the playground on a sunny day. You will be asking children to apply the sorting and classifying skills they learned indoors to a larger setting.

Skills and Concepts

- sorting
- classifying
- comparing

What to Do

1. Children tend to transition better to a new activity if they have a purpose that holds their attention along the way. Before transitioning out to the playground, give each child a small paper bag for collecting nature items.

2. Introduce the plan by saying, "Today when we go outside to play we are going to first look for some interesting objects such as stones, fallen leaves, bark, or seed pods and place them in our bags. Then when we are playing outside we can sort all the things we found just like pirates sorting their treasure! Ready, pirates? Let's see what we can find!"

3. After children have completed their treasure hunt, have them dump out their "loot" and notice similarities and differences among the items.

4. Provide a collection of boxes, tubs, or trays into which your young pirates can sort their treasures. Easy ways to begin sorting include by size (big and little treasures), color, and shape.

Variations

 Sing a Pirate Song: Add a pirate treasure-hunt song to the transition activity.

"Pirate Treasure Hunt"
(sing to the tune of "The Wheels on the Bus")

The pirates on the hunt
Go looking around
Looking around
Looking around
The pirates on the hunt
Go looking around
At the playground.

Leaves and twigs all
Go together
Go together
Go together
Leaves and twigs all
Go together
Because they're brown.
[Repeat the second verse, changing the words to sing about other treasure hunt items.]

How Many? How Much? Pirates like to know how much loot they have found. Ask children to count the number of objects in each pile and compare. Ask questions to spark their thinking—for example, "Which pile has the most treasures in it?" "Which pile is the biggest? Smallest?" "Does biggest mean more?" "Why do you think so?" "How many objects do we need to add to each pile to make all the piles equal?"

Small, Medium, Large

Have you ever noticed how young children love to play with empty containers? Sometimes the container is as much fun as what's inside! With this activity, exploring container sizes creates a natural transition to another part of the day.

Skills and Concepts

- measuring
- classifying
- matching
- comparing
- small-motor development
- vocabulary development

What to Do

1. Gather a collection of small, medium, and large containers and lids. Give a container (no lid) to each child.

2. Invite children to compare their container with their neighbor's. You might ask, "How are your containers different? How are they the same? Can one fit inside the other? What do you think?"

3. Help children to use the math vocabulary words *small*, *medium*, and *large* by asking them to hold up their container if they think it is small (or medium, or large). Encourage children to help one another decide what size their container is by comparing it with others. Interestingly, one container might appear large next to a small container but medium next to another, larger one!

4. Place the lids in the center of the circle. Have children take turns choosing a lid for their container. If they make an incorrect choice, they can return the lid and wait for another turn. Once children have a matching lid, they can transition to the next activity.

Variations

Help Your Neighbor: Invite children to find the matching cover for a neighbor's box instead of their own.

What Goes Inside? Play the game again, this time replacing lids with objects that match the boxes in size. Have children find the object that goes in their box—for example, a medium object for a medium box.

What Goes With What?

An important part of sorting is an understanding of relationships among objects. In this matching game, children transition by sorting objects based on the way they are used together.

Skills and Concepts

• sorting
• matching
• recognizing attributes

What to Do

1. Place pairs of everyday objects (such as brush/comb, toothbrush/toothpaste, shoes/socks, soap/washcloth) in a bag or box. Include enough objects for every child to have one.

2. Pass the bag around the circle and have each child randomly take one item.

3. Discuss each item and how it is used. Then have children find a classmate who has an object that makes a pair with theirs. Encourage children to discuss with their partners why their objects go together. How would they use them?

4. Following the discussion, send pairs off as transition partners for the day! Choose other partner-based transition activities throughout the day, such as Number Line Buddies (page 68) and Estimating Partners (page 72).

Variations

● **Go Together:** Extend the experience by making sets of "Go Together" cards using pictures from magazines or catalogs—for example, clothes/dresser, food/refrigerator, snow/boots, peanut butter/jelly, and desk/chair.

● **Long Ago and Now:** Make picture sets featuring items that were used long ago and those commonly used today—for example, horse and buggy/car, candle/lamp, ice block/refrigerator, and washboard/washing machine.

Shape Treasure Hunt

As you excuse children to transition, send them on a shape treasure hunt. The special focus will help them move from place to place in an organized way.

Skills and Concepts

- observing
- comparing
- matching
- counting

What to Do

1. Make shape viewers: Cut circle-, rectangle-, and triangle-shaped windows in index cards (one window/shape per card). Glue the index cards to craft sticks.

2. Give each child a viewer. Have children use their viewers to look for particular shapes. Children with square-shaped viewers find squares in the room. Those with circle viewers find circles, and so on.

3. When children find a matching shape they can put a shape sticker on it and make a tally mark on a record sheet. How many shapes did they find?

Variations

Shapes Lead the Way: Take the shape treasure hunt around the school. For example, look for shapes on the way to the cafeteria. Affix shape stickers on the way to the destination and retrieve them and place on a graph on the return trip.

Outside Shapes: If you are transitioning to the playground, take the viewers and tally sheets with you and make them available for children to use during outdoor recess. Compare indoor and outdoor tallies at your next circle time. Which place has the most circles? Triangles? Squares?

Ask the Number Puppet

Skills and Concepts

• sequencing

• ordering

• inferencing

With practice, young children can begin to understand and use the order of numbers in a sequence. Here is a simple and fun guessing game you can use in a transition moment to develop this skill.

What to Do

1. Choose a simple hand puppet to be the class "Number Puppet." (For fun and effect, you can decorate the puppet with a hat, scarf, or tie covered in numbers.) Hide the puppet inside a decorative bag with a hole in the bottom so you can put your hand through both the bag and the puppet.

2. Introduce the game by saying, "Hiding in this bag is a new classroom friend, Number Puppet. Number Puppet loves all the numbers from zero to ten but will only come out of the bag when it hears the secret number for the day. Do you think we can guess the secret number? What number do you think we should ask about?" [Accept ideas.] "Okay, let's test it out by counting to [first number guess] and see what happens."

3. When the puppet does not come out, children can then suggest another number. If the number is closer to the secret number, the puppet can begin to poke its head out of the bag (but not all the way) as children count to that number. This is a clue that the number is closer to the second guess than the first. You might ask, "Who can think of a number that is between our two guesses?" Try counting to that number. If the number is correct, the puppet can come out of the bag and take a bow and congratulate all the children! The puppet can then lead children in a celebratory counting song that goes up to the secret number of the day. (If the number is not correct, continue leading children through the process of identifying numbers between their guesses to eventually guess the correct number.)

Variations

• **Secret Number of the Day:** Use the secret number throughout the day. Have children take that many giant steps to the door, count out that many pretzels for snack, or use that many shapes or colors in an art project.

• **Puppet Patterns:** The Number Puppet can also create patterns (for example, clap, tap, clap) for children to guess and try out themselves. Children can also create patterns for the puppet to try.

Hands and Feet

Children's hands and feet lead the way in sorting and patterning activities that are perfect for times the class is transitioning from one activity to another.

Skills and Concepts

* sorting
* patterning
* sequencing
* seriating

 ## What to Do

1. Provide construction paper (half sheets) in several colors. Help children trace their hands and feet on construction paper, one hand/ foot per sheet. Have children write (or help them write) their names on each hand and foot tracing.

2. Use the tracings for sorting and patterning activities. As children place their tracings according to the sorting or patterning rule (see below), they can move on to the next activity.

   • Sort all the hands into two groups: thumbs facing left and thumbs facing right.

   • Sort by color: all red hand or foot tracings in one group, all blue in another, and so on.

   • Clip pairs of hands and/or feet on a clothesline in seriated order from small to large (or the reverse).

   • Rearrange the hands (or feet) on the clothesline into a repeating color pattern such as yellow, blue, yellow, blue.

   • Arrange hands and feet to create a hand and foot color pattern such as red hand, blue foot.

Variations

Hands-On Numbers: Assign children a number to write on their hand tracings—for example, from 1 to 5. Let children sort hands by number—all the 1s in one pile, the 2s in another, and so on. Or, have children sort hands into groups to create sets with one of each number.

Numbers and Names: Let children sort their hand and feet tracings by number of letters in their names. Hands with two letters go in one pile, three letters in another, and so on.

What Comes Next?

Skills and Concepts

- patterning
- sequencing
- recognizing shapes and colors

Simple patterning activities with shapes and colors can be used as a quick time-filler or a transition activity to move children off to the next event!

What to Do

1. Cut out shapes from sturdy paper as follows: ovals and circles in one color; squares and rectangles in a second color.

2. Display the shapes and ask: "What do you notice about the shapes? How are the ovals like the circles? How are the squares like the rectangles?"

3. Model the activity by creating a simple starter pattern of shapes and/or colors for children to continue. Start the pattern and have children tell what comes next.

4. Now children are ready to use the shapes in a transition activity. Invite a child to be the "Pattern Leader." This child chooses several shapes to begin a pattern. Children in turn choose a shape to continue the pattern as they leave the group and transition to the next event.

5. Repeat the activity with other transitions (same day and on other days) to give everyone a chance to be the Pattern Leader.

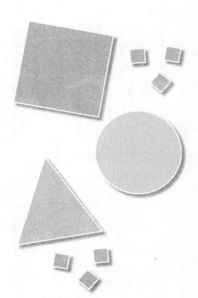

Variations

- **On My Own:** Make the shapes available throughout the day and encourage children to mix and match the shapes to create patterns of their own.

- **Seasonal Shapes:** Vary the shapes, incorporating shapes that are connected to seasons— for example, use different leaf shapes in the fall, snowflake shapes in winter, and flower shapes for spring.

Paper Chain Transitions

Once children contribute a link to a colorful paper-chain pattern, they transition to the next activity.

Skills and Concepts

* patterning
* sequencing
* measuring

 What to Do

1. Prepare a collection of, say, red and blue paper strips (approximately 2 by 8 inches). (Or substitute other colors.) Make at least four strips per child so that you have enough for many versions of this transition game.

2. Give each child one paper strip. Explain, "We are going to make a paper-chain pattern by alternating two colors. Red, blue, red, blue…what comes next?" (Create the first three or four links as you model the process.)

3. Have a child with a red strip thread the strip through the last link you made, form the strip into a circle, and tape or staple the ends to secure. This child then proceeds to the next activity.

4. Then have a child with a blue strip attach his or her strip to the previous link, and then move on to the next activity.

5. Repeat for remaining children, alternating between the two colors to continue the pattern. Once children have added their strip to the paper chain, they proceed to the next activity.

6. At the end of the transition, hold up the chain for all to see! Place the chain in the math center for children to use as a measuring device. Encourage their explorations, asking: "What can you find that is the same length as our transition chain?"

Variations

● **Add a Color:** After children have mastered the two-color pattern, add more colors or change the repeat in the pattern. For example, try making a repeating green, blue, blue, yellow pattern.

● **Measuring Tools:** Keep the transition chains in the math area for children to use as units of measure throughout the year.

Walk the Seriation Line

Skills and Concepts

- observing
- comparing
- measuring

Seriation, the process of ordering things in a particular order (such as from small to large), helps children understand the values of numbers in the number line. Have children line up in size order and then reverse!

What to Do

1. Have children stand in a line and notice the person to their right. Is that child the same height, shorter, taller?

2. Have the child who is shorter move to the right. Now look again. Is the person to your right shorter? Continue making adjustments until everyone is lined up with the shortest person on the right and the tallest to the left. Time to march off in a seriation line. Here is a song to take you there.

Teaching Tip

You may have to help children at first, but each time they line up this way, they'll strengthen their seriating skills.

"When the Kids Go Marching In"
(sing to the tune of "When the Saints Go Marching In")

Oh, when the kids go marching in
Oh, when the kids go marching in
We're marching down in size order
Oh, when the kids go marching in.

Variations

- **Small Group Seriation:** To simplify this activity, divide the class into small groups. Have children organize themselves in size order within their groups. When children are ready, combine two groups and repeat.

- **March, Skip, Hop:** As a variation on the song, have children substitute words for other ways to move (in place of *march*) and perform that movement as they sing their new version of the song and transition from one place to another.

Bigger Than a...

Children place objects on a line in size order as they get themselves in line.

Skills and Concepts

• comparing
• seriating
• measuring
• describing

What to Do

1. Tape a length of adding machine tape on the floor or a table to create a seriation line.

2. Place a tiny object (such as a counter) at one end of the line, and a large object (such as a telephone book) at the other end. This will help children visualize the range of the seriation line.

3. Place a collection of different-size objects, such as books, boxes, crayons, and spoons in a bag or box.

4. Have a child pull out one of the items and describe its size. You might ask, "Is it big or little, tiny or giant?" Have the child place the object anywhere on the seriation line. The child then lines up for the next activity.

5. Have the next child select another object and describe its size. Ask: "How is it different from the first object? Which object is bigger? Where would you place this on the seriation line?" Have the child place the object on the line, using the previous object as a clue, and then proceed to get in line. Continue the game until all children have added an object to the seriation line and joined their classmates in line.

Variations

● **Bigger, Smaller:** Encourage children to verbalize the seriation line by pointing to each object of increasing size in turn and saying, "This [book] is bigger than this [block]." Then reverse direction to reinforce the concept of "smaller than."

● **In the Bag:** Give each child a bag in which you've placed a single item. Have children look at the item in the bag, and then identify a classroom object that is bigger or smaller. Let children share their findings ("This pencil is bigger than the crayon in my bag"), then return objects to their places and trade bags to play again.

Domino Send Off

Children use giant dominoes in a game that leads the way to a calm and purposeful transition. Plus, children will be using essential patterning skills as they play!

Skills and Concepts

• counting

• matching

• patterning

What to Do

1. Make giant dominoes out of cardstock. Cut the cardstock into uniform rectangles, with the length being double that of the width (6 by 12 inches each is a good size). Draw a line to divide each rectangle in half to form two square ends. Draw a set of from one to six dots on each half, as with traditional dominoes. (Or use colorful stickers, such as stars.) You can leave some ends blank to represent the concept of zero. Make an even number of domino halves for each number (so children can match them up). Six or eight of each works well.

2. When you are ready to transition, give each child one domino. Explain that when children place their domino correctly in the game, they are excused from the group.

3. Begin by modeling how to join two or three dominoes edge to edge. Ask if anyone has a domino that matches either end of the dominoes you have connected. Have children take turns adding their domino to the line, and then send them off with a big hooray!

Variations

• **More Than One:** If you have more time, give each child more than one domino. When children have placed all their dominoes, they move on to the next activity.

• **Shape Dominoes:** Instead of dots to represent numbers, draw a shape on each domino half. Have children join dominoes by matching shapes.

Clap and Chant a Pattern

Skills and Concepts

- patterning
- sequencing
- listening

It is important to take the process of mathematic patterning beyond visual patterns by asking children to use verbal and auditory patterning skills as well. This transition activity invites children to explore patterning through a multisensory approach.

 **What to Do**

1. Create simple, two-part patterns for children to "read" together. For example, you can have half the class stand up and create a boy, girl, boy, girl pattern. Have remaining children read the pattern together from one end of the line to the other, clapping their hands as they chant the words (*boy, girl, boy, girl,* and so on). Let children trade places and repeat.

Boy Girl Boy Girl Boy

2. Now invite children to create more complicated patterns to read, clap, and chant. Send children around the room to find items they can use to create a pattern. Different types of math counters, blocks, or art supplies are useful. They might create, for example, button, button, chip, button, button, chip.

3. Have children read their patterns together, clapping as they chant the words. Once they are comfortable with the words, you can ask them to create a more regular, rhythmic chant.

Variations

- **Clap, Snap, Tap:** Have children choose a clap, snap, and tap combination to go with each pattern. Children might, for example, clap for buttons, snap for chips, and tap for blocks.

- **Auditory to Visual**: Challenge children to think in reverse. Display objects for creating patterns. Use sound to create a pattern (such as clap, snap, clap, snap). Have children arrange the objects to show the pattern they heard.

The Case of the Missing Pattern

Skills and Concepts

* sequencing
* patterning
* observing
* problem solving

Here's an intriguing whodunit for children to solve using patterning skills. Use this to provide a short interlude between other events or to provide a warm-up to a math lesson.

What to Do

1. Use simple math counters or classroom materials to create patterns with missing pieces. Start by laying out a long, simple, two-part repeating pattern such as crayon, block, crayon, block, and so on. Leave out pieces throughout the pattern. You might leave a space to provide a clue that something is missing.

2. Explain to children that you need their help to solve the mystery of the missing pieces. Ask them to put on their thinking caps and look to see what is missing, and where. Just for fun, you can pass out real or pretend magnifying glasses to add a "Sherlock Holmes effect" to the investigation.

3. Once children identify what's missing, have them place the objects in position to complete the pattern. Eventually children will become so adept at this game that they can be the "robber" and create the "What's missing?" patterns for others to solve.

Variations

🔹 **More Complex:** Repeat this game frequently using more and more complex patterns. Try variations such as three- or four-part patterns using similar objects. Or make a pattern based on color but not object, such as red ball, yellow paper, red crayon, yellow block.

🔹 **Change Direction:** Create patterns that include objects in unexpected position—for example, a triangle block pointing to the left or right. These sorts of positioning changes challenge children to develop important visual discrimination skills that help them recognize differences between numerals and letters.

Hop Right In

Is it hard to get children to come in from the playground? Make the transition inside something to look forward to with this hopscotch game!

Skills and Concepts

- counting
- sequencing
- large-motor development
- taking turns

What to Do

1. Draw a simple hopscotch game on the sidewalk right in front of the door to the building. Number the squares 1 to 10 (see right), making the last two squares (9 and 10) lead right to the door so that children can hop right in!

2. When it is time for children to head back into the building, call a few of them at a time to hop their way in. Encourage children to count the squares as they go.

Variations

Hop and Chant: Create a hopscotch chant to go with this transition.

> One, two
> Hop my shoe.
> Three, four
> Touch the floor.
> Seven, eight
> Don't be late!
> Nine, ten
> Inside again.

Numbers and Counting: Draw dots (or other small objects, such as stars) in each space on the hopscotch board to represent the corresponding numeral.

Number Words: Replace numerals on the hopscotch board with number words (or show both).

Tell a Kitten Number Story

Skills and Concepts

- counting
- adding and subtracting
- one-to-one correspondence

Got a few transition minutes to fill? Tell a number story to pass the time and to introduce adding and subtracting in a hands-on way! An excellent way to introduce number stories is to use children as the "things" to be counted.

What to Do

1. Ask for five children to volunteer to act out a story as you tell it. It is helpful to have some props to get children into their roles. For this story about cats, make five paper-plate "kitten masks" for children to use (see right). Provide hats or scarves for children playing the remaining roles (people looking for kittens).

2. Distribute the props and begin the story:

> Once upon a time there were five kittens living together in one big house. Let's count them: one, two, three, four, five. They loved to run and climb and play with one another all day long. At night they all cuddled together—one, two, three, four, five—in one big ball. One day someone came knocking on the door looking for a kitten for her daughter. She looked and looked at the kittens and took one away. Now how many kittens are left? One, two, three...four! Now four kittens played and played together until there was a knock on the door. In walked three people looking for kittens. They played with the four kittens and each took one. How many kittens are left? One! The one little kitten was feeling pretty lonely and sad until there was another knock at the door. The first kitten came back to visit and now there were how many kittens? One, two! The first kitten's owner decided she really needed two kittens, and so she took both kittens home. How many kittens are left? None. Zero!

3. If time allows, repeat the story to allow a new group of children to act it out.

Variations

- **On Our Own:** Make the props to the story available for children to retell and dramatize the number story independently. Record the number story for children who want to act it out with the props as they listen.

- **Kittens, Puppies, and Goldfish:** Change the story by adding more kittens or changing characters (and props) to puppies or goldfish!

One Banana, Two Banana

Skills and Concepts

- counting
- adding and subtracting
- one-to-one correspondence

Transition time is a great time for an adding and subtracting rhyme. Use a classic counting-off game with a new set of words to introduce some fun with adding and subtracting.

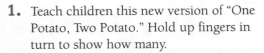 **What to Do**

1. Teach children this new version of "One Potato, Two Potato." Hold up fingers in turn to show how many.

> One banana, two banana, three banana, four.
> One jumped and it fell to the floor.
> How many bananas are left? Three.
>
> One banana, two banana, three bananas now.
> One skipped away and took a bow.
> How bananas are left? Two.
>
> One banana, two banana, stand up tall.
> One sprouted wings so it wouldn't fall.
> How many bananas are left? One.
>
> Sad little one banana, standing all alone.
> Feeling so lonely, she called on the phone,
> "Two banana, three banana, four banana come,
> To play with me and have some fun."
> How many bananas now? Four!

2. Recite the rhyme together, inviting children to hold up their fingers to show how many bananas.

Variations

- **Puppet Props:** Children can make puppets to act out the rhyme. Provide banana-shaped templates. Have children trace, cut out, and color four each. Glue bananas to craft sticks. Have children use their bananas to show how many as they recite the rhyme.

- **Banana Hats:** Make simple banana hats children can wear to "be" the bananas in the rhyme. Make a crown to fit each child's head and top with a yellow banana cutout. Let children take turns in groups of four acting out the rhyme.

Counting Fish

Skills and Concepts

- counting
- adding and subtracting
- one-to-one correspondence

If you have a few transition minutes to fill, children can practice adding and subtracting with this "extended play" version of the familiar song "I Caught a Fish Alive."

What to Do

1. Most children are familiar with the classic song "I Caught a Fish Alive." But you can also hum the tune for children to spark their memory. Invite them to hum along the second time through.

2. Now you are ready to introduce the new words to the song. Show children how to use their fingers to represent the fish.

   One, two, three, four, five
   I caught five fish alive.
   Six, seven, eight, nine, ten
   I add five fish again.

   How many do I have?
   Ten little fishies on both hands!
   Five fishies swim away.
   How many are left today?

Variations

- **How Many Fish?** Repeat the song several times, each time changing the number of fish that swim away in the second verse.

- **Make a New Song:** Let children suggest other creatures to replace the fish in this counting song. For example, they can count butterflies or bugs. Change the word *swim* accordingly (to *fly*, *crawl*, and so on).

So Many Friends!

Skills and Concepts

- counting
- adding and subtracting

A new version of a familiar tune lets children kinesthetically experience adding and subtracting as they are excused from circle time.

What to Do

1. Teach children the following song, based on "Johnny Works With One Hammer":

   Johnny takes one friend, one friend, one friend,
   Johnny takes one friend, now there are two.

   Johnny takes two friends, two friends, two friends,
   Johnny takes two friends, now there are four.

   Johnny takes three friends, three friends, three friends,
   Johnny takes three friends, now there are seven.

   Johnny takes [four, five, and so on].

2. Ask one child to volunteer to be Johnny (or the leader). Sing the song and let the leader take the appropriate number of children from the circle as the song progresses.

3. Continue until all children are in line with Johnny/the leader and ready to go.

Variations

- **Sing a New Name:** Personalize the song by singing the leader's name instead of *Johnny*.

- **Add an Ending:** As you guide children away and transition them to the next activity, sing this new ending to the song:

   Johnny drops off two friends, two friends, two friends,
   Johnny drops off two friends, now there are [the number of children remaining].
   Continue taking two children away and counting the remaining children until just Johnny is left.
   Then sing, "Bye, Johnny!"

Five Little Pelicans

How does a pelican fly? Here is a great subtraction rhyme for finding out! Try this activity to give children a movement break at the beginning or end of circle time.

Skills and Concepts

- counting
- subtracting
- large-motor development
- one-to-one correspondence

What to Do

1. Invite children to share what they know about pelicans. If possible, show children a picture of this majestic seabird.

2. While sitting in a circle, choose five children to be pelicans. Give each a number card to hold, on which you've written the numerals 1 through 5 (one per card).

3. While the other children recite "Five Little Pelicans" (see right), the pelicans take turns flying away, circling once around the group as the children sing and then coming back to "roost" in their original spots by the end of the verse. (Children can remain standing and quietly "flying" in place until all children have had a turn and you are ready to move on to the next activity together.)

4. Give the cards to five new children and repeat. Continue until all children have flown away and come back to roost. Then move on together to whatever is next.

Variations

🔵 **Away We Go:** Recite the rhyme several times as a means for dismissing children from the group. Start with five pelicans and send each off to the next activity instead of back to their roost. Repeat until everyone is excused.

🔵 **Choose a New Bird:** Let children suggest a new bird to use in this rhyme. You might share a nonfiction book about birds and let them select a favorite. One day they might be tiny hummingbirds, on another day, tall, graceful cranes.

"Five Little Pelicans"

Five little pelicans
Sitting on the floor,
One flew away
And then there were four.

[chorus; repeat after each verse]
Pelican, Pelican
How do you fly?
Strong and slow
You stay in the sky!

Four little pelicans
Sitting in a tree,
One flew away
And then there were three.

[chorus]

Three little pelicans
What do they do?
One flew away
And then there were two.

[chorus]

Two little pelicans
Basking in the sun,
One flew away
And then there was one.

[chorus]

One little pelican
Sitting all alone,
It flew away
And then there was none!

Five Little What?

What would happen if the five little speckled frogs in the classic counting rhyme turned into elephants? Find out in this silly adding and subtracting rhyme. Use it to fill a few minutes, provide a fun break between activities, or to excuse children a few at a time from an activity.

Skills and Concepts

- counting
- adding and subtracting
- fine-motor development

What to Do

1. Invite children to recite the rhyme "Five Little Speckled Frogs." Encourage them to add hand motions to represent the frogs and the action in the song.

"Five Little Speckled Frogs"

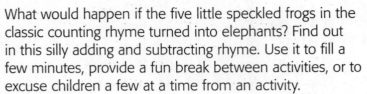

Five little speckled frogs, [Hold up five fingers (frogs).]
Sat on a speckled log, [Place fingers on other arm (log).]
Eating the most delicious bugs. Yum! Yum!
One jumped into the pool, [Move one finger off your arm.]
Where it was nice and cool.
Now there are four green speckled frogs. [Hold up four fingers.]
[Repeat for four, three, two, and one.]

2. Ask children what they think would happen if the frogs turned into elephants. What would the water in the pool look like after they went in? Then sing a new version, creating motions to illustrate the actions (see right).

Variations

- **New Numbers:** Change the numbers to challenge children's counting skills.

- **Add and Subtract:** Try taking away more than one or adding one and have children tell how many there are.

"Five Messy Elephants"

Five messy elephants,
Sitting on a great big fence,
Needing a most delicious bath. Glub! Glub!
One jumped into the pool,
Where it was nice and cool.
Now there are four elephants. Glub! Glub!

Four messy elephants,
Sitting on a great big fence,
Needing a most delicious bath. Glub! Glub!
One jumped into the pool,
Swimming like a messy fool.
Now there are three elephants. Glub! Glub!

Three messy elephants,
Sitting on a great big fence,
Needing a most delicious bath. Glub! Glub!
One dove into the pool,
He forgot the strict pool rule.
Now there are two elephants. Glub! Glub!

Two messy elephants,
Sitting on a great big fence,
Needing a most delicious bath. Glub! Glub!
Both jumped into the pool,
Playing a game so cool.
Now there are how many elephants?
None! None!
Now there is one big messy pool. Yuck! Yuck!

The Kids Go Marching

New lyrics to a familiar song will get children up and moving. Use it as a transitional action break or as a means to move children from one place to another.

 ## What to Do

1. Sing the original "The Ants Go Marching" song together as a tuneful reminder. Then introduce the new words (right) and ask children to move as directed by the words. For example, in the first verse, they march single file. In the second, they pair up and march with a partner. In the third, children march three abreast, and so on.

2. Continue the song as far as you like, giving children plenty of time between each verse to reconfigure the number in each set.

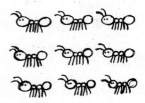

"The Kids Go Marching"
(sing to the tune of "The Ants Go Marching")

The kids go marching one by one
Hoorah, hoorah.
The kids go marching one by one
Hoorah, hoorah.
The kids go marching one by one
The little one stopped to wiggle his thumb.
And they all go marching around the classroom,
To keep on counting.

The kids go marching…
[Continue with "two by two," "three by three," and so on through "ten by ten," maintaining the rhyming language of the original version or substituting your own rhyming lines as desired.]

Variations

- **More Ways to Move:** Change the word *marching* to invite children to move in other ways. For example, they can go skipping, dancing, or tiptoeing.

- **Rhyming Fill-Ins:** Stop before the end of line six in each verse and let children suggest a new way to complete the rhyme—for example, "The kids go marching three by three/the little one stopped to . . . scratch his knee." Nonsense words are fine, too!

Tell a Fishy Number Story

Skills and Concepts

- counting
- adding and subtracting
- one-to-one correspondence

Using props with number stories provides excellent hands-on practice with adding and subtracting. Use this game as a transition to snack time or as a midday snack break because children will be eating their subtractions!

  What to Do

1. Give children eight edible counters, such as goldfish crackers, raisins, or grapes. (Check for food allergies first.)

2. Ask children to pretend that their left hand is the great big ocean. Have them add and take away fish in the ocean as you share this story:

> Once upon a time in the great big ocean there lived five little fishies. Can you put five fishies in your ocean? The fish loved to swim around and around playing on the waves. Then one day two more fish came to play. Can you add two more fish to the ocean? Now how many fish are playing together? Yes, seven! One day four fish swam away to a faraway reef. Can you take away four fish? [Children may eat them.] How many fish are left in the ocean? Yes, three! The other fish continued to play together, riding the waves and diving for food. Then one day a new fish came to play. Can you add one more fish to your ocean? How many fish are in the ocean now? Yes, four! The fish told their new friend about their old friends at the reef. "Do you want to go see them?" they asked. "Yes," their new friend said. The four fish swam off together. [Children take away four fish, eating them if desired.] How many fish are left in the ocean now? Yes, zero!

Variations

- **More Fish Friends:** Change the number of fish in the ocean (providing more crackers as necessary).

- **Animal Cracker Counting:** Use animal crackers rather than goldfish and change the story accordingly.

The Countdown-to-Vacation Chain

Skills and Concepts

- counting
- subtracting
- comparing

As you well know, children get very excited when they know it's almost vacation time. Here is a concrete way to help children anticipate and transition to these special times in a constructive way. They will be getting wonderful practice in subtraction, too!

What to Do

1. Use a class calendar to count the number of school days until vacation time.

2. Provide each child with colorful 1- by 9-inch paper strips.

3. Have children add a link to their personal chain for each day of school that remains until vacation time, writing their name on the first link. Display the chains in the circle time area. Children might enjoy drawing a favorite vacation picture to place at the end of their chain.

4. Each day, have children remove one loop. How many days of school until vacation time now?

Variations

- **More Countdowns:** Children can make countdown chains during their birthday month to show how many days until it's their birthday.

- **Count-Up Chains:** Reverse the activity and have children add a link each day leading up to vacation time. How many days have gone by? How many days left?

Measure It!

Estimating how much or how many is an essential part of learning how to measure. Use this activity to practice nonstandard measurement when transitioning from one place to another.

Skills and Concepts

- counting
- estimating
- measuring
- comparing
- more than, less than, equal to

What to Do

1. Before transitioning to another activity or place, ask children to estimate how many regular steps, giant steps, tiptoes, or twirls it will take to get there. For example, you might ask, "How many giant steps to the playground? How many tiptoes to the snack table?"

2. Record children's estimates, then measure. As children participate in this activity, it is important to use and reinforce comparative math vocabulary and concepts. Help children notice measurements that are more than, less than, or equal to their estimates. Eventually, children can express how many more or less the estimate is from the actual measurement.

Variations

- **Playground Math:** After estimating, then measuring, how many steps to the playground, let children further explore measurement. As units of measure, provide classroom materials such as blocks and rulers, as well as outdoor materials such as hoops and balls. Ask, "How many blocks [hoops, balls] long is the swing set?"

- **Measuring Sticks:** Encourage children to explore making measurements using a variety of natural materials, such as sticks, leaves, and rocks. They can measure everything from the sandbox to the tire swing. What do children estimate is the longest item on the playground? Measure and see!

Feather Race

Time to move the group on to another activity? This race will have children very focused as they try to move a feather the fastest.

Skills and Concepts

- estimating
- counting
- measuring
- evaluating
- comparing

What to Do

1. Give each child a straw and a feather (cotton balls also work well). Ask children to estimate how far they can blow the feather in one breath. Have them use their hands to show their estimated distance.

2. Let children test blowing through the straw to move the feather. Have children notice the different directions the feathers go in just one breath.

3. After children have discovered how far they can make the feather go on one breath, they are ready to go the distance. Give children a transition destination (such as the activity tables or the door) and ask them to estimate how many breaths it will take to get the feather there. Record their estimates.

4. Have children count how many times they blow into the straw to move their feather. (Or pair up children and have one count while the other moves the feather. Later in the day, repeat this activity and have children trade places so everyone gets a turn with both parts.) How close were the estimates to the results?

Variations

Just One: Instead of blowing through the straw to move the feather from one place to another, have children experiment with how far they can move it in one breath.

More to Move: Compare blowing into the straw to move a feather with moving other objects, such as a paper clip or a table-tennis ball. What is easier or more difficult about moving each object?

A Measuring Treasure Hunt

Children learn measurement skills best when they explore the process of measurement with nonstandard tools. They don't need a ruler or a yardstick because they can always use their hands!

Skills and Concepts

- measuring
- observing
- matching
- estimating
- comparing

What to Do

1. Send children on a measuring treasure hunt around the room. Have them hunt for something that is the same size as their hand. Model the activity first by placing your hand next to an object and asking if your hand is the same size, bigger, or smaller. Repeat for several objects to demonstrate that some objects might be bigger or smaller, and that you will continue to measure until you find one that is the same size.

2. Once children have the idea, they can go off on the hunt. Have them collect their findings and bring them back to the group to share.

3. Arrange children's objects in a line. Ask questions to guide a discussion—for example, "What do you notice about these items? How are they the same? How are they different?" "Can you organize them in a row from smallest to largest? Which item do you think is smallest? How can we tell?"

Variations

- **Bigger, Smaller, Just Right:** Vary the hunt by having children find one object that is smaller than their hand, one that is bigger, and one that is the same. Encourage them to use math vocabulary for size as they share their findings.

- **Handprint Measurement:** Children might enjoy making a finger-paint handprint on paper and cutting it out to use as their own standard of measurement. When the paint is dry, have children write their names on their handprints. Laminate (or cover with self-adhesive clear vinyl) and trim to size. Clip handprint measures to a clothesline in the math area for easy access. Children can freely use these whenever they want to measure something. How many hands tall is the block tower? How many hands long is the jump rope?

The Longest Paper-Clip Chain Ever

Skills and Concepts

* measuring
* counting
* cooperating
* fine-motor development

Sometimes the goal in a transition is to move children in a slow and organized way. Paper-clip chain making is just the right kind of quiet and methodical activity to both calm and interest children.

What to Do

1. Fill a container with large paper clips. Demonstrate how to attach one paper clip to another. Children can work quietly on their own chains and then combine them to make a long chain. Or they can all work together on a giant chain, taking turns adding the paper clips.

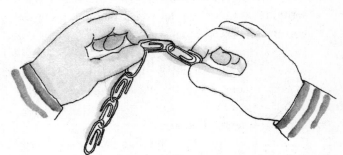

2. Ask questions as children work—for example, "How big do you think we can make our paper-clip chain? Can we make it as long as the [rug, table, room, hall]? What can we find that is the same size as our chain?"

3. Let children use the chain as a unit of measure, using it to find something that is the same length, shorter, or longer.

Variations

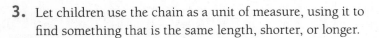

Ever-Growing Chain: Place the chain in the math center for children to freely use as a unit of measure. Encourage children to add to the chain whenever they need a quieting activity.

Long, Longer, Longest: Invite children to consider the longest thing they can measure at school. Then let them use the longest paper-clip chain ever to measure it! Revisit this activity as children continue to add to the chain from day to day. Discuss how the measurement changes as the chain length grows.

How Far Will It Go?

Children love windup toys. Use them for this challenging and fun estimation experiment. This activity provides a playful or fun time filler when you have a few extra minutes.

Skills and Concepts

- estimating
- comparing
- measuring
- evaluating
- more than, less than, equal to

 What to Do

1. Bring in a collection of windup toys for children to explore.

2. Use tape to make a start line on the floor. Have children estimate how far each toy will go before it stops. Children can write their name on a piece of masking tape and use it to mark their estimated spot.

3. Have children wind up their toys (holding them in place) and position the toys on the start line. When you say "Go" have children release their toys.

4. Have children use tape in a different color to mark the distance their toy went, and then compare their estimate with the actual distance. Ask questions that encourage math vocabulary—for example, "Is the distance more than or less than your estimate?"

Teaching Tip

Leave a "start" line on the floor so children can test their windup toys at a moment's notice.

Variations

- **On a Roll:** How do children think the distance traveled by a toy car or truck they push will compare with that for the windup toys? Let them test their ideas, again using tape to mark estimates and actual distances. Compare results. Which toys go farther? Why?

- **Incline Comparisons:** Add a new dimension by taking the activity outside to test on an incline plane such as a hill or the slide.

Measure With Me

Need a quiet, calming activity? Send children on a measuring hunt to find things that are the same size as they are.

Skills and Concepts

- measuring
- matching
- one-to-one correspondence
- seriating

What to Do

1. Gather ribbon, adding machine tape, and thick yarn for use as measuring tapes. Children will cut these measuring tapes to match their height, so start with lengths that are at least a bit longer than the tallest child. Invite children to choose one form of measuring tape to use.

2. Working in pairs, have children help each other cut a length of their selected measuring tape to match (approximately) their height. Have children label their tapes. They can write directly on the adding machine tape, or tape a name tag on the ribbon or yarn.

3. Let children use the measuring tapes to find things in the classroom that are just their size. Give children sticky notes to label with their name the objects or places they find. Take time to let children share their findings with you. (You might do this over the course of the day.)

Variations

- **Seriated Order:** Let children arrange their measuring tapes in seriated order (for example, they might tack them to a bulletin board at their height, tape them to a wall, or clip them to a clothesline in the classroom). Keep these available for children to use independently.

- **Taller or Shorter?** Pose problems for children to explore with their measuring tapes. For example, ask, "Can you find something taller [shorter] than you?" or "What can you find that is equal to two of you [your measuring tapes]?"

Picture Cube Graphing

Skills and Concepts

- counting
- graphing
- comparing
- recognizing quantities

Children's pictures on milk-carton cubes invite irresistible, instant graphing opportunities that are just right for transitioning from one place, such as circle time, to another.

What to Do

1. Make a class set of graph markers: Glue each child's photo on one side of a clean, dry school-size milk carton. Cover with clear contact paper. Tape down the top to create a cube.

2. Use the cubes to create picture graphs whenever you have a few minutes to fill. Start by graphing boys and girls. Distribute the picture graph markers to their owners. As children are transitioning to the next activity have them stack their cube in either the "girl" or "boy" tower.

3. When children return to the area for the next group activity, invite them to read the graph. You might ask, "Which tower has the most cubes [or is taller]? Are there more boys [girls] than girls [boys]?"

Variations

More Graph Markers: Instead of using milk cartons for graph markers, try gluing photos to small, uniformly sized gift boxes. Or, tape photos to blocks. Consider using anything children can stack.

More Graphing Topics: Children can use their cubes for endless graphing experiences. For example, they can use the cubes when they arrive at school to create an attendance graph. Or, they can use the cubes to graph votes, such as for a read-aloud book or recess game.

The Ice Cream Graph

Circles and triangles make an excellent pictorial ice-cream graph that children can create as they transition to a new activity.

Skills and Concepts

• counting

• estimating

• graphing

• number recognition

 What to Do

1. In advance, cut out construction-paper circles in different colors to represent ice cream flavors. Cut out construction-paper triangles to represent cones. Tape a row of cones along the bottom of a sheet of chart paper. Label each cone with a different flavor ice cream (include as many as you like). To provide a visual clue, write labels in colors that correspond to the ice cream flavors. Use Velcro or removable wall adhesive to make this a reusable graph.

2. As children prepare to transition to a new activity, invite them to select a "scoop" that represents their favorite flavor ice cream. Have them vote for this flavor by placing the scoop on the corresponding cone. How many scoops does each cone have?

Variations

🍦 **More Favorites:** Use simple shapes to create other pictorial graphs. Try voting for favorite colors, shapes, foods, books, or songs.

🍦 **Block-Builders' Graph:** Children transitioning from the block area can make graphs as they prepare to put blocks back where they go. As children take down towers and other block structures, have them graph the blocks they used by size and shape (arranging blocks in rows or columns on the floor). Which type of block did they use most of? Fewest of?

Count on Me Graph

Kids love to play with sticky notes. Use them to create a very personal graph! Use this activity to provide an active transition to whatever is next.

Skills and Concepts

- counting
- one-to-one correspondence
- graphing

What to Do

1. Set up a simple bar graph on a sheet of chart paper, dividing the paper into five to ten columns. Label each column along the bottom with a drawing of a different body part (such as arm, leg, head, hand, foot, knee, eye, nose, mouth, and ear). Use a different color for each picture, and have sticky notes (or sticky dots) available in these colors.

2. Have children place small sticky notes on their bodies in the colors that correspond to each part. (If possible, take a picture of children all covered with stickies!)

3. Have children notice which parts they have just one of and which parts come in pairs or twos.

4. Have children take turns transferring the stickies to the graph in the appropriate columns as they're transitioning. When they're finished, they can move on to the next activity.

Variations

Add a Rhyme: Teach children a rhyme to go with the activity.

I've got one head, one mouth, one nose.
Ten little fingers and ten little toes.
Two hands, two feet, two eyes and knees
It all adds up to a wonderful me!

Add Labels: Label the pictures on the graph and pre-label sticky notes to reinforce vocabulary for body parts.

What My Body Can Do Graph

Children use estimating and graphing skills to create this very active graph, perfect for those times when children need a movement break.

Skills and Concepts

· estimating
· counting
· graphing

What to Do

1. Set up a graph to show how many times children can perform an action, such as hopping. (See sample, right.)

2. Invite children to predict how many times they can perform the action. Record their predictions and then test them out.

3. Graph results, having children color in a square to show their count. Note: To simplify the activity, remove the numbers on the y-axis and have children count the shaded boxes to tell how many children hopped one time, two times, and so on.

Variations

🔹 **Skip and Snap:** Make a new graph and try another action. Skipping and finger snapping are fun, too!

🔹 **How Many in a Minute?** Introduce concepts of time by graphing how many times children can perform an action in a minute (or some other period of time, such as 30 seconds).

Graphing Zero and More

Skills and Concepts

• counting
• graphing
• comparing
• sorting
• concept of zero

Bar graphs are a good way to help children begin to understand the concept of zero in relationship to numbers of things. Use this simple graph as a quieting transition when children need to focus and calm down.

What to Do

1. Gather collections of objects, such as a handful of pompoms, marbles, counters, or buttons. Make sure the items in each set are several different colors—for example, red, blue, yellow, and green counters.

2. Set up a graph with names for colors across the bottom and the numbers 0–10 on the left. Include all colors represented by the objects, plus one color that is not in any collection of objects. Label each color. Laminate the graph for durability if desired.

3. Let children sort the materials by color onto the graph, and then count and tell how many of each color, including in the zero set. Note: To simplify the activity, remove the numbers on the y-axis and have children count boxes to find out how many of each color.

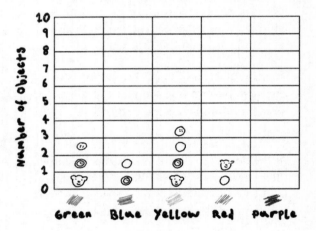

Variations

Sorting Sacks: Place sets of objects along with corresponding graphs in bags. Children can select a bag to sort and graph, and then return the materials to the bag when finished. These portable sorting and graphing centers are perfect for a child who finishes an activity early or for choice time. To reinforce the concept of zero, include on the graph one color that is not represented by any object in the set.

Category Sort and Graph: Organize collections of objects around categories such as Nature, Shapes, or Touch (children can sort and graph objects by the way they feel—for example, soft, scratchy, or squishy).

Take a Color Survey

A color survey of the room is a very purposeful (and colorful) way to transition.

Skills and Concepts

- observing
- matching
- tallying
- counting
- graphing
- comparing

What to Do

1. At transition time, give each child a sheet of primary-colored paper. Use a variety of colors, including black, white, and brown. Distribute paper so that there are a few children for each color.

2. Tell children that their job is to go around the room looking for objects that are the same color as their paper. Show children how they can make a tally mark on the paper for each object they find. They can also include a simple drawing.

3. Define a place in your meeting area where children can place their survey sheets when they are finished and are ready to proceed to the next activity.

4. At the next group time, have children collect their sheets and compare their surveys with one another. Show children how to count the tally marks by fives.

5. Sort surveys by color, and then graph results. Compare results for each color.

Variations

🌀 **Sticker Match:** Give children stickers in different colors. Invite them to place the stickers on items around the classroom that match. Once children have finished placing their stickers around the room, have them gather the stickers and arrange them by color in rows on chart paper. Guide a discussion about the data—for example, ask, "How many red things did you find in the room? Blue? Which color did we find the most of? Fewest of?"

🌀 **Cleanup Color Graph:** As children clean up at the dramatic play center or other area, invite them to sort items before putting them away. Make a basic bar graph on chart paper (draw lines to divide the paper into five to eight columns), and laminate. To sort by color, place a different-color crayon at the bottom of each column. Let children sort their items by color before returning them to their places.

Month-by-Month Transitions

Children come to school with certain skills and abilities that grow and change throughout the year. But we all know that the months and seasons affect children, too. In December, for example, children are often excitable. During other months, such as February, they may need to be energized and inspired. The activities in this section of the book provide different types of transitions for different times of the year. These transitions were created with a sensitive eye to the needs of children in an effort to anticipate the types of transition activities that may be most effective each month. For example, September has activities to encourage sharing with new friends, while June has activities to celebrate the year collectively.

> ## Teaching Tip
>
> As you use the transition activities in this section, you'll find several repeating components, including:
>
> - seasonal celebrations
> - treasure hunts
> - relaxation activities
> - movement games
> - imaginary trips (excursions of the mind)
>
> Invite children to recall activities that are similar to one they are about to try. Revisiting familiar ideas can help strengthen skills and build confidence.

Of course, this doesn't mean that an activity can and should be used only in the month it is offered. It is important to revisit activities throughout the year. Each time children encounter a prior activity, they bring to the experience the expanded skills and knowledge they've gained along the way. In this way, children further develop and deepen their skills and learn to apply them to new sets of circumstances. Please use these activities liberally throughout the year. Apply your own creative touches and, most of all, have fun. Remember, transitions are brief moments in time, to be cooked up with great big dollops of humor!

Transition Leader's Hat

Skills and Concepts

- taking turns
- leadership
- listening
- observing

As you know, September transitions can be the time when your organization and routine fall apart. This is partly because children are just getting to know one another and have not learned how to take turns being both leaders and followers. September is a good time to introduce this concept with a wild and wacky prop, the Transition Leader's Hat!

What to Do

1. Create a wonderfully wild and crazy hat for the transition leader to wear. You can use a baseball cap or a cardboard cone as a base and add fun materials such as feathers, pipe-cleaner spirals, glitter, and streamers—whatever will get children's attention!

2. It is best for you to wear the hat first. This will tweak children's interest and get them excited about their turn to wear it. Plus, you will also be modeling how to be a transition time leader.

3. You can pretend to be the Pied Piper, put on the hat, wave your hands, and invite children to march behind you in line.

4. In time, turn the hat over to children, who can take turns being the transition leader.

Variations

Sing a Leader Song: As you march children from one place to another, sing this song to the tune of the Mickey Mouse club song.

> Who's the leader of the group?
> To go from here to there?
> [Leader's name] is! [Leader's name] is!
> With hands up in the air!

Transition Leader's Cape: As a variation on a leader's hat, jazz up a cape for the transition leader to wear. Start with a simple cape. Let children all lend a hand in decorating the cape with fabric paint, sequins, ribbon, and other craft supplies.

Cue It Up!

Every good ensemble needs some cues now and then. Your class is no exception. Start the year off right by creating visual and auditory cues that will keep your transitions (and kids!) moving smoothly.

Skills and Concepts

- listening
- following directions
- cooperating

 What to Do

1. How many ways can you get children's attention? As many as the number of signals you create! Introduce the concept of cues by providing children with experiences with different types of signals. You first might want to experiment with different sound signals such as a *swoosh* across a xylophone, a strong drumbeat, a ringing bell, or chords on a piano. During the first few weeks of school, try one type of cue throughout the day.

2. Have children practice freezing and listening for directions whenever they hear the sound. You might say, "When you hear the xylophone, freeze whatever you are doing and look at me for directions." Children love the idea of freezing, so practice freezing and unfreezing several times!

3. At the end of the day ask children to rate the signal on a scale of 1 (low) to 5 (high). Compare the ratings at the end of the month and choose a few favorites to use consistently. But save the other sound signals for later in the year when the original one no longer works!

Variations

- **Visual Cues:** After experimenting with sound signals, move on to visual cues. Try hand motions, sign language, blinking the lights, or turning off the lights and shining a flashlight around the room like a spotlight.

- **Make My Pattern:** Instead of having children freeze on a signal, teach children a clapping pattern that signals them to stop and listen. When they hear you clap this pattern, they stop what they're doing, repeat the clapping pattern together, and then listen for your direction.

Buddy Up!

One of the first rules children need to learn in the beginning of the year is how to move smoothly from one activity to another throughout the day. A buddy system makes it doubly fun.

Skills and Concepts

- following directions
- understanding routines
- cooperating
- social interaction

What to Do

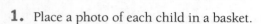

1. Place a photo of each child in a basket.

2. Each day at group time, have children draw a photo from the basket to see who their buddy is for the day. They can then return the photos to the basket.

3. When you give the transition signal (for example, by ringing a bell), have children quickly find their buddy and listen for instructions!

Teaching Tip

You might want to practice this strategy a few times so children understand the concept. For example, make the transition signal while children are at choice time and have them find their buddy and freeze in place. When everyone has their buddy, give a cheer and ask them to do a few quick movements together. Then send them off to continue their choice time activity. Repeat this several times during the week until children can buddy up without confusion.

Variations

Where's My Buddy? Sing a song to signal children to find their buddies.

"Where's My Buddy?"
(sing to the tune of "Are You Sleeping?")

Where's my buddy? Where's my buddy?
Here I am. Here I am.
We are buddies today. We are buddies today.
You and me. You and me.

Buddies Clean Up: After children have learned how to transition from one activity to another with their buddy, add the buddy-up system for cleanup time!

The Birthday Leader

You can make children feel special on their birthday by identifying them as the transition leader for the day.

Skills and Concepts

- self-esteem
- taking turns
- leadership

What to Do

1. The first birthday of the year is a good day to introduce a special song and game. You might introduce it by saying, "We have a friend in class today who is celebrating his birthday. To make the day feel special, we will make our birthday friend the transition leader for the day. Here's a song to do it!"

2. Sing the birthday leader song together a few times, and then invite the birthday child to take his or her role as leader.

"The Birthday Leader Song"
(sing to the tune of "Twinkle, Twinkle, Little Star")

Happy Birthday to our friend,
[child's name] is [child's age] today.
Please stand up and take a bow.
You can be our leader now.
Happy Birthday to our friend,
[Child's name] is [age] today.

Variations

- **Spin Around:** Some children may prefer not to be the leader and should be allowed to pass on the opportunity. Just sing the song and change the fourth line to "Spin around and sit down now."

- **Birthday Buddy:** Invite the birthday child to select a birthday buddy to help lead the class throughout the day.

How Many Ways Can You Move?

Skills and Concepts

- following directions
- large-motor development
- taking turns
- creative thinking

Sometimes the hardest part of a group activity can be the ending! In September, children need help moving from the end of one activity to the beginning of the next one without too much confusion and stress. Adding a creative movement encourages children to focus their attention on the process of moving in an organized and playful way as they transition from here to there.

What to Do

1. Introduce this transition by asking, "How many ways can you move across the room?" Invite children to share ideas. If children are having difficulty suggesting movements you can say, "We can slither, crawl, slide, walk, skip, jump (on one foot or two), and spin. What other ways can we move?"

2. Explain: "We need to go from circle time to the activity tables. Who can suggest a fun movement to get us there?" Each day have one child be the transition movement initiator. That child chooses a movement for the others to use throughout the day whenever there is a transition from one place to another.

Variations

○ **Movement Chart:** Record each movement leader's name along with his or her movement on a chart. If possible, include a picture as a visual clue. Children can refer to it during the day as a reminder. Once each child has had a turn choosing the movement, you can start over again with the first child and his or her movement! (Or let children choose new movements.)

○ **Surprise Movements:** Write names for different movements on slips of paper, add a picture if possible, and place in a hat or bag. Each day, let the movement leader choose a slip to find out what the movement for the day will be.

Transition a Go-Go

Children may have been in school for a while now, but they often still need help organizing themselves during transition time. A song is one of the best ways to get children moving in a happy and organized way to the next activity. When you use something with a familiar tune, such as "Bingo," you have an instant winner!

Skills and Concepts

- listening
- receptive language
- name recognition
- taking turns

What to Do

1. Teach children these new words to "Bingo." In each of lines 3, 4, and 5, insert a different child's name. Change the ending according to where children are lining up.

2. Once children are familiar with the words, sing it together to excuse children from a group activity or circle time. Point to each child excused in turn, so the class can join you in singing their names in lines 3, 4, and 5.

"Transition a Go-Go"
(sing to the tune of "Bingo")

There was a teacher had a class
That's always on the go-go
[Child's name] you may go
[New child's name] you may go
[New child's name] you may go
And line up at the door-o.

Variations

- **Transition Leader:** You can use this song with the Transition Leader's Hat activity (page 113). Invite the first child named to put on the "leader hat" (or cape) and lead remaining children in lining up as they are called.

- **Clap, Snap, Tap, Stomp:** Invite children to join in clapping, snapping, tapping, or stomping the syllables in each child's name as she or he is excused in the song.

Crayon Cooperation

One way to have the children learn about one another as they transition from an activity is to have them create a cooperative picture together.

Skills and Concepts

• taking turns
• creative expression
• small-motor development
• cooperating

What to Do

1. Place a large sheet of mural paper on a table. Tape corners in place.

2. When you are ready to excuse children from a group activity, such as circle time, give each child a crayon.

3. As you excuse children one at a time, invite them to make a quick shape, line, or drawing on the paper. To make the activity even more cooperative, use only one crayon and have each child pass it to the next child to be excused. Children add on to the drawing until everyone has had a turn and the picture is complete.

Teaching Tip

Children can be invited to connect their drawing to something already on the paper or begin something new on the paper.

Variations

More to the Masterpiece: If children like, pull out their cooperative picture at another transition time and let them continue to add to it until they feel their masterpiece is complete.

Add a Story: Display the completed picture. Invite children to give it a title and then write a class story about it. Add the title and story to the display.

Weather Reporters

Skills and Concepts

- observing
- predicting
- vocabulary development

In the first few months of school, children's attention span for circle time activities is short and there just isn't enough time to do everything from taking attendance to talking about the weather. Consider reorganizing parts of your circle time activities to transition times throughout the day. Children are better able to pay attention during these shorter periods of time. October is a good month to begin collecting weather information for the year. Use this activity to move weather from circle time to transition time.

What to Do

1. Prepare a simple weekly weather graph (see right). Provide picture symbols children can paste in each column.

2. Keep the chart ready for any short transition time you have throughout the day. An excellent choice is the very last one of the day before children make the transition home.

3. Have one child be the weather reporter for the day and add a weather symbol (sun, cloud, raindrop, snowflake) to the weekly chart.

Variations

🌀 **Weather Journal:** At the end of the month, transfer the information to a weather journal. Revisit the journal throughout the year to compare the weather each month. How is January different from June?

🌀 **Temperature Graph:** Have children create symbols that indicate the day's general temperature. Is it hot, warm, cool, or cold? (Children can suggest other words to indicate the temperature, too.) Graph this in addition to, or in place of, "sunny, cloudy, rainy, snowy."

Use Your Senses

From the sight of leaves turning colors to the crunch of a fresh-picked apple, the month of October is a sensory-rich time of year. Encourage children's sensory awareness with a transition activity that invites them to explore their surroundings, one sense at a time.

Skills and Concepts

* expressive language
* creative thinking
* vocabulary development
* visual perception
* sensory awareness

What to Do

1. Choose a sense to focus on—for example, sight. Model the activity by completing this sentence frame: "My eyes see _____." Fill in the blank with something you see. Include a word or two to describe it—for example, "My eyes see a yellow leaf."

2. As children prepare to transition from one activity to another, have them take turns completing the sentence frame, and then moving to the next activity. If children are having difficulty thinking of a describing word just ask them to name the object.

3. If time permits, ask a follow-up question to elicit a describing word—for example, "What do you notice about the shape of [what the child named]?"

Variations

🍂 **More Than One:** Give children the option of using more than one word to describe what they see. Record children's ideas on separate sheets of paper, to be illustrated at a later time, and put the pages together to make a class book.

🍂 **Touch and Hear:** After children are familiar and comfortable with using the sense of sight, change the transition topic to another sense, such as touch or hearing ("My hands feel…" "My ears hear…").

We're Going to the Firehouse

October is fire safety month. If you can't get to a real firehouse, you can take this imaginative field trip together right in your own classroom. You can use this story/chant as a transition activity all month to bring children together for a group activity or to move them from one place to another. By the end of the month, children will think they really were there!

What to Do

1. Introduce a new version of the classic language game "We're Going on a Bear Hunt." To begin, gather children in a seated circle. Have children tap a steady beat on their legs as you recite a "call and response" chant together (see right). Have children repeat each line after you say it.

2. After reciting the rhyme a few times, invite children to add appropriate hand motions to go with the words/actions. For example, children can act out getting on the bus, opening the door to the firehouse, and climbing up the ladder.

3. Continue with verses about related topics—for example, the fire truck, a firefighter's clothing/hat, the hose, and so on, ending with taking children back to the bus and to school.

Variations

From Here to There: To use this activity to move children from one place to another, change the last verse to match their destination—for example, "Oh, look! What's that? It's the playground. Can't go around it. Can't go under it. Gotta go in it! All ready? Let's go!"

More Imaginary Field Trips: Take imaginary field trips to other fall destinations, such as an apple orchard or a pumpkin patch.

Skills and Concepts

- creative dramatics
- following directions
- listening
- creative thinking
- small- and large-motor development

"We're Going to the Firehouse"

(chant to rhythm of "We're Going on a Bear Hunt")

We're going to the firehouse.
All ready?
Let's go!
Climb on the bus.
Drive away.
Goodbye, school!

Oh, look!
What's that?
It's the firehouse.
Can't go around it.
Can't go under it.
Gotta go in it!
All ready?
Let's go!

Oh, look!
What's that?
It's the ladder.
Can't go around it.
Can't go under it.
Gotta go up it!
All ready?
Let's go!

It's Fall

By November in many places, leaves on many trees have changed colors and are falling. Animals may be preparing for winter. You can prepare your class, too, with this simple and fun "finger play." Use the finger play throughout the month whenever you need an activity to quiet children and get their attention.

Skills and Concepts

- expressive language
- vocabulary development
- taking turns
- counting

What to Do

1. Copy the verse at right on chart paper. If possible, add drawings that represent the hand motions. Read the rhyme with children.

2. Repeat the rhyme, this time having children hold up fingers to show how many birds, acorns, mice, and so on. Have them act out the action in each verse—for example, flying away like the bird in verse one and falling to the ground (as an acorn) in verse two.

Variations

Sleepy Bears: Change the verses to add rhymes about what happens with other animals in the fall. For example, "four hungry squirrels" might become "four sleepy bears."

New Fall Finger Plays: Invite children to help you make up new versions of the rhyme about other things that happen in fall months. For example, they can do a Thanksgiving rhyme featuring "one fat turkey, two baked breads, three cans of cranberries, four baked pies, and five mashed potatoes." End the rhyme with "It's Thanksgiving!"

"It's Fall"

One little bird,
Ready to fly.
Off for the winter,
Says goodbye.

Two tiny acorns,
Fall from the tree.
Will the mice find them?
Let's just see.

Three chubby mice,
Gather up the nuts.
Yes, they found them,
Hiding in ruts.

Four hungry squirrels,
Searching for food.
Stash it all away,
In the neighborhood.

Five falling leaves,
Red, orange, brown.
Sail down, down, down
To the ground.
It's fall!

Morning Mailboxes

November is a good time to revisit September's Buddy Up! activity (page 115) and help children continue to get to know their classmates and learn to recognize their names. Using mailboxes during transition times is a way to practice names and make connections that will continue to make children feel part of the community throughout the day.

> ### Skills and Concepts
>
> - visual discrimination
> - name recognition
> - cooperating

What to Do

1. Use a hanging shoe bag to create mailboxes for children. Write their names on labels and place them on the pockets. Add a simple symbol or sticker for each child. It is a good idea to have children choose their own symbols. They will learn their symbol very quickly because it is a representation of "me."

2. On 3- by 5- index cards glue an extra set of symbols; these cards will serve as the "mail" children will receive in their mailboxes. Before children arrive at school, place a different symbol card in each mailbox, matching partners to ensure they get each other's cards. For example, if Evie has a card with Kobie's symbol, make sure Kobie has Evie's card.

3. At the end of circle time, have children check their mail. The index card/symbol in their mailbox tells them who their transition partner is for the day. To do this, they have to match the symbol to the friend's mailbox and read the name! Offer support as needed, but with daily use, children will quickly learn to read one another's symbols and names.

Variations

🌀 **Jobs in the Mail:** Use the mailboxes to assign classroom jobs. Assign each job a symbol and make a corresponding set of "job" cards—for example, a picture of a fish for feeding the fish. Place the job cards in children's mailboxes. (Make and distribute multiple cards for jobs that require more than one helper.) When it is time to transition to these activities (classroom jobs) children can check their mailbox to find out what to do.

🌀 **Friendly Notes:** When children want to send a note to a friend, they can find the friend's symbol, copy the name, draw or write their message, and then place it in the mailbox.

An Arty Idea

Skills and Concepts

* creative thinking
* brainstorming
* problem solving

From leaf rubbings to nature collages, fall is a time that inspires many art projects. This "art bag" helps children transition to art activities while providing direction and warming up creative thinking skills.

What to Do

1. In a bag, place art supplies for a project you have planned. For example, you might stock a bag with fall leaves, paintbrushes, paper, glue, crayons, and jars of paint.

2. Say to children, "I have a problem. I have all these things to use at the art table today and I can't remember what we were going to do with them. Do you think you can help me?"

3. Pass the bag around the circle and invite children to feel and guess the contents. Ask questions to guide their thinking—for example, "What do you notice about these items? What are some things you can do with them?" Let children take turns removing some of the items for further examination. Ask: "What do you think we could make with these?"

4. Write children's ideas on chart paper. When it is time for children to transition to the art table, they will have many ideas from which to choose!

Variations

🌀 **How Many Ways?** Encourage children to notice the many ways they used the same art supplies. Did some children paint around the leaves, leaving a leaf shape in the white space? Did some make leaf rubbings? Maybe others traced leaves and colored them with bright, fall-color crayons.

🌀 **Corn on the Cob Creations:** Corn is a fall staple. Stock a bag with ears of corn (husked), paper, polystyrene trays, and paint. Ask children how they think they could use the corn like paintbrushes. (Roll an ear in the paint, and then roll it on paper.) What can they make using the corn and painting in this way (gift wrap, place mats, patterns)?

Sing a Song of Transitions

By November your original transition songs may not be working quite as well as they did at the beginning of the year. Here is a new one to add a fresh dimension to the fun. Introduce it at the beginning of the week and by Friday children will have added it to their repertoire of transition songs.

Skills and Concepts

- following directions
- listening
- creative expression

 What to Do

1. Copy the song "Sing a Song of Moving" (see right) on chart paper. Sing it with children several times for practice.

2. Repeat the song until children have found a partner and arrived at the next activity. (Combine this with Buddy Up! (page 115) to pre-assign partners for the day.

"Sing a Song of Moving"

(sing to the tune of "Sing a Song of Sixpence")

Sing a song of moving
Going here to there.
We all listen wisely
To get us there with care.

First we find a partner
Then we're on our way.
What a very happy thing
To get us there today!

Variations

- **Where Are We Going?** You can change the generic second line of the first verse to name where children are going—for example, "Going to the gym" or "Going out to play." Try to keep the number of syllables the same as in the original line (five).

- **Carefully, Alertly, Attentively:** Invite children to suggest new words with a similar meaning for *wisely* in line three. Try them out!

Thankful Transitions

Skills and Concepts
- expressive language
- cooperating
- creative thinking

November is the month for expressing gratitude. Give your November transitions a Thanksgiving focus by asking children to express what they are thankful for before going off to the next activity. This creates a warm and loving way to excuse children.

What to Do

1. Introduce the activity by modeling how to express something you are thankful for. You might say, "I want each of you to tell me someone you are thankful for. I will go first. I am thankful for all of you, because being here with you makes me happy. Who are you thankful for?" (Begin by having them think of people they are thankful for.)

2. Invite children to raise their hands when they can think of someone they are thankful for. Call on them and offer a sentence they can complete: "I'm thankful for...." You may have to help children with this at first but if you repeat this activity several times during the month children will get more comfortable with the idea and will be able to think of many ways to complete the sentence.

Variations

🔵 **Going Further:** After children have begun to understand the concept of gratitude, you can invite them to suggest things they are thankful for as well as people. Be open to all their ideas no matter how odd they may sound. Remember, they are communicating their feelings and they need to feel safe to express them.

🔵 **Send Thanks:** As a class, think of someone in the school you are thankful for. As children are excused from an activity, let them take turns telling why they are thankful for this person. Record their thoughts on chart paper in the form of a letter and deliver it to the recipient.

A Recipe for Moving

Skills and Concepts

- following directions
- listening
- creative movement

Thoughts of December bring the sensory delights of cooking up favorite holiday foods. You can use the format of a "recipe" to create this simple and fun movement game to get children moving from one place to another. At the same time you will be giving children practice with following directions.

What to Do

1. Have children brainstorm favorite holiday foods. List their suggestions on chart paper.

2. When it's time to transition from one place to another, choose a food from the list and use it to create a "recipe for moving." To create the recipe, make up simple commands in recipe format for children to move to as they transition—for example, here's a recipe for Banana Bread:

   Mash the bananas. [Children make mashing motions.]

   Mix in flour and sugar. [Children turn around and around.]

   Pour yourself into a pan. [Children stand up and pour themselves forward.]

   Slide yourself into the oven and bake! [Children slide toward the door (or other location).]

Variations

- **Pop, Pop, Pop:** A favorite is the recipe for popcorn because children get to pop, pop, pop to the next activity.

- **Follow the Leader:** Eventually children will be able to choose a food from the list and lead their classmates in a recipe for moving.

Look at This!

Skills and Concepts

- focusing attention
- observing
- expressive language

As you well know, without children's focused attention, group activities can be a challenge! It is helpful (and fun) to create simple and quick transition activities that encourage children to focus on you—especially at a time of year when distractions may be greater than usual. This simple idea uses the element of surprise to get children's attention.

What to Do

1. In a bag or pillowcase place an unusual object, such as a peacock feather, a beautiful flower, or a huge leaf.

2. When you feel like you are losing children's attention, reach in the bag and pull out the object. Just the surprise alone will get their attention!

3. Once you have children's attention, go further by inviting them to quietly look at the object. You might say, "Try looking at the object from different directions, from above and below. Keep looking at it until you notice a surprise, or something you never saw before."

4. Let children take turns sharing their thoughts. Write children's observations on chart paper so that they can also see what their words look like in print.

5. After children have participated in the observation game they may like to incorporate the surprise object into their playtime (if appropriate).

Variations

🌀 **Contents to Consider:** Children respond well to all sorts of surprises, including small stuffed or wheeled toys, a magic wand, a beautiful shell, a sparkly rock, even a fresh fruit or vegetable!

🌀 **Surprise Box:** Use fancy boxes or gift bags to keep several attention-getting surprises on hand. Keep them close to your circle time area for use when children need a change of pace during this time.

A Colorful Treasure Hunt

Skills and Concepts

- observing
- matching
- visual discrimination

December is a month of holidays filled with color and light—a perfect time for a colorful treasure hunt! Treasure hunts provide for engaging transitions from one activity to another, giving children something to focus their attention on as they take a fun break. This one lets children hunt for samples of colorful holiday paper.

What to Do

1. Discuss colors children see in the world around them. You might ask, "What colors do you see at this time of year? Where do you see them? Do we have any holiday colors in our room?"

2. Collect a variety of colored papers (such as tissue paper and gift wrap). Try to find two different papers for each child. Keep a sample of each paper and then hide the papers around the room.

3. Have each child choose two paper samples. Then send children on a treasure hunt around the room to find the papers that match theirs. Have children bring their paper treasures to the art table.

Variations

- **Colorful Collages:** Let children use the paper to create colorful holiday collages. Encourage children to experiment with tearing and cutting the paper into different sizes and shapes.

- **Create a Card:** Children can use the collages they make as artwork for colorful holiday cards.

Let's Face It

December is a time of many feelings for children, most of them intense. With all the December holiday excitement, it is a good idea to have a few activities that channel children's energy in a positive way. This one also helps them just relax and have fun despite the flurry of commotion that might be going on in the world around them.

Skills and Concepts

- following directions
- sequencing
- taking turns
- observing

 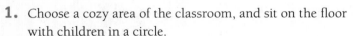 **What to Do**

1. Choose a cozy area of the classroom, and sit on the floor with children in a circle.

2. Explain how to play a "faces" game. You might say, "I am going to make a funny face and pass it to the person next to me. That person will make the same funny face and pass it to the next person until we go all the way around the circle. Can we do it? Sure!"

3. Begin with an easy face to replicate, such as a silly smile or a look of surprise. Then turn to the child on your right and make the face. That child makes a face just like yours and turns and passes it to the next child in the circle, and so on.

Teaching Tip

Don't worry about how well children replicate the face. This is more about relaxing and having fun with a silly activity than about doing something perfectly. In fact, some of these faces are so funny that children are bound to be giggling by the end of the circle, getting them ready to tackle the next part of their day with good humor.

Variations

Your Turn: Invite children to take a turn making a face to start the game. They can try happy, funny, even sad or angry faces. Children will feel comfortable expressing these different emotions within the safe confines of the game. Plus they get to see the "mirror" of the emotions in the faces of others.

Faster Faces: After children get the hang of this activity, try passing the faces faster and faster. This is an excellent way to use up some of those "high" December energies in a constructive way. Just remember to end with a slow one! For another change of pace, just pass the face in the opposite direction.

New Year's Resolutions

Skills and Concepts

- creative thinking
- using imagination
- creative dramatics
- large-motor development

Adults make New Year's resolutions in January, and children can, too. Resolution making can last all month long if you use it as a quiet discussion transition or waiting-time activity.

What to Do

1. Discuss the idea of New Year's resolutions. You might say, "In the beginning of a new year, some people like to think about what happened last year and what they would like to change, improve, or accomplish. For example, someone might decide to eat healthier foods. In the new year, people make resolutions to do these things. A resolution is like a promise. What would you like to work on at school this year? What is your resolution?"

2. Write children's ideas on separate sheets of paper and add their names. You will probably be able to do this with just a few children at a time, so it is good to spread the activity over a month.

3. During activity time, give each child his or her paper to illustrate.

4. Children can take their papers home to share with families, but keep a classroom copy for use at the end of the month. At this time, check in with children to see how they are doing.

Variations

🔵 **Chart It:** Turn this activity into a math experience by creating a chart of the simple resolutions that are easy to tally. For example, children can add a tally mark each time the group feels they had a successful circle time, or did a good job cleaning or lining up. This is a group decision so everyone has to agree!

🔵 **Class Resolution:** In addition to or in place of individual resolutions, invite children to work together to decide on a class resolution. What is something children as a group would like to work on? Set a goal and revisit it weekly to help children notice their progress.

Take an Imaginary Trip

In many parts of the country, winter can bring a longing for travel to warmer places. If your class experiences cabin fever, use creative movement and drama to take an imaginary trip that will calm and center children. This activity is just right for a mini-transition break between activities.

Skills and Concepts

- creative thinking
- using imagination
- creative dramatics
- large-motor development

What to Do

1. Ask children: "If you could go anywhere, where would you go?" Write their ideas on chart paper and have children choose a group destination.

2. Brainstorm ideas for taking a trip to the beach, a park, anywhere! For example, if children want to go on a camping trip, ask: "What would we need to bring with us? How would we get to the campground? What would we do when we arrived?"

3. Lead children on the imaginary trip, pantomiming together each step of the way—for example, packing camping gear, hiking into the campsite, unpacking the tent, setting it up, and hammering in stakes. Don't forget to have a pretend campfire, "roast" some marshmallows (you could bring in real ones for a special treat), and sing camp songs!

Teaching Tip

You might want to gather some props to enhance a variety of imaginary experiences. Sunglasses, hats, scarves, and bags can be useful for a trip to almost anywhere!

Variations

Endless Vacation: Invite children to continue their imaginary vacation at the dramatic play area. Their vacation can go on for days and days!

A Day at the Beach: When cabin fever hits again, change the location and act out going to the beach. Remember to pack the beach towels, sunscreen, and beach balls. Put on sunglasses and a cap and you're ready to go!

Do the Limbo!

Make a warm Caribbean theme part of your winter transitions with a limbo game that builds exercise and fun into getting from one place to the next.

Skills and Concepts

- large-motor development
- taking turns

What to Do

1. The object of the game is for children to slide under the stick without knocking it down. Use a broomstick or some other type of thin pole.

2. Have two children lightly hold the stick about waist height in the air and invite children to line up behind it. Then have them go under the stick, one at a time. If the child is able to get under it without knocking it down, he or she can go to the end of the line and continue playing. If the child misses, then he or she proceeds to the next activity.

3. After everyone in the group has had a chance to go under the stick, lower it for a greater degree of challenge. Continue in this way until the stick is too low for anyone to pass under.

Teaching Tip

You might want to play some island music to add to the fun. Children who are in line waiting can swing and sway or clap to the music.

Variations

- **While You Wait:** If the next activity is something the group is doing together, designate an area for children to gather once they have knocked down the stick and are waiting for the others to join them.

- **Creative Movement:** Invite children to create different ways to go under the limbo stick. Can they lean backwards to go under the stick? Slide their way through?

The Children in the Dell

By January, children are comfortable in the group and are ready to participate in a cooperative movement game. This is the perfect time to introduce an interactive transition song and dance. Here is one with a tune that needs no introduction!

Skills and Concepts

- listening
- following directions
- large-motor development
- cooperating
- patterning

What to Do

1. Use the familiar tune and pattern of "The Farmer in the Dell" to create a transition game to lead children from one activity to another. Begin by having children stand together in a circle and hold hands.

2. Sing the first verse and have children circle around and around.

3. As you sing the second verse, have one child join hands with another, and then together circle once around the outside of the circle and go off to the next activity. Continue until all children have had a turn and are successfully transitioned.

"The Children in the Dell"
(sing to the tune of "The Farmer in the Dell")

The children in the dell,
The children in the dell,
Hi-ho, the derry-o,
The children in the dell.

[Child's name] takes [child's name] hand,
[Child's name] takes [child's name] hand,
Hi-ho, the derry-o,
[Child's name] takes [child's name] hand.

Variations

🌙 **Many Ways to Move:** Invite each pair of children to choose a way to move around the circle and off to the next activity—for example, they can skip, spin, or slide. Change the words to the song accordingly: "[Child's name] slides with [child's name]," and so on.

🌙 **Inside the Circle:** For a version that simply provides children with a movement break (and does not excuse them in pairs to the next activity), have one child stand in the center of the circle as others circle around and sing. This child then chooses a child to join him or her, while everyone sings, "[Child's name] chooses [child's name]." As you sing the next verse, that child takes the next child from the circle, and so on, until everyone is in.

Cats and Dogs

February is a time of year that often finds children restless, making this a good month to introduce yoga-inspired activities. Children really seem to respond to these activities. Perhaps it is the calming and centering quality of the postures or the playful imitation of animals and things. Whatever it is, yoga works for creating a quick transition activity that settles children down and channels their physical energy in positive ways!

Skills and Concepts

- listening
- following directions
- using imagination
- large-motor development

What to Do

1. Invite children to pretend to be cats. Have them kneel on all fours, hands under shoulders, and then give them a minute to explore different cat-like movements.

2. Guide children through a cat-like pose. You might say, "What does a cat do when it sees a dog? Yes, it arches its back. Let's pretend that we are cats. Take a deep breath, and round your back up to the ceiling like this. Let your head hang down. Hold this position as you breathe deeply through your nose. I will count 1-2-3-4 for the in breath and 1-2-3-4 for the out breath. Then we'll rest."

3. Now invite children to be a dog. Say: "Go back on all fours and roll your head back and up. Hold this position as you breathe deeply through your nose. I will count 1-2-3-4 for the in breath and 1-2-3-4 for the out breath. Then we'll rest."

4. After children have experienced both the cat and dog positions, they can alternate between them.

Teaching Tip

Some yoga postures resemble animals such as cats and dogs. These visual images make the postures both easy and fun for young children to follow.

Variations

- **Sound Effects:** At the end of the session, allow children to choose to be either a cat or a dog and transition to the next activity as they make the movements and sounds of that animal.

- **More Animal Movements:** Other animals like to stretch. Invite children to use their imagination and create some other animal stretches for their classmates to try.

A Valentine's Transition Game

Get your children in the mood for Valentine's Day by using this transition game all month. They will soon be wearing their hearts on their sleeves!

Skills and Concepts

- cooperating
- sharing
- creative movement
- large-motor development

What to Do

1. In advance, prepare pairs of matching cardboard hearts of different sizes, shapes, and colors. Make armbands by stapling a circle of elastic cord to each heart cutout. Children will wear the hearts as armbands for this game. Also choose a selection of suitable music to play during the game.

2. Introduce the game by showing children the hearts and asking them to help you find the matching pairs. You can do this by helping them notice the differences and similarities in the hearts.

3. To play the game, place the heart armbands in a decorative bag. Demonstrate how to take a heart armband and place it on your arm. Then let each child randomly select and put on an armband.

4. Guide children in playing by saying: "As soon as you have a heart on your sleeve, go find an open place to stand in the room and wait for the music to start. When it starts you can move to the music until it stops. Then find your partner by matching your hearts. When the music starts again, you and your partner can move together. But the next time it stops, you and your partner will move to the next activity."

Variations

Single Attribute Match: To simplify the game, have children pair up by matching hearts that share one attribute—for example, color. Make each pair of hearts a different color.

Letters and Numbers: Create a version that encourages letter recognition. Write uppercase letters on one set of hearts and lowercase letters on another set. Children find partners by matching upper- to lowercase. Or, reinforce counting by having children match the number of dots on their hearts.

Shadow Movement Break

Skills and Concepts

* creative movement
* large-motor development
* eye-hand coordination

February is a time when children may not get outside enough to express their energy in fun and constructive ways. Bring the outside in with an active transition game that uses children's natural interest in light and shadows.

What to Do

1. Turn off all or some of the lights and use a large flashlight or projector to shine a light across the room and onto a facing wall. Play some quiet instrumental music and invite children to move with their backs to the light.

2. Ask questions to inspire imagination in children's movements: "What do you notice on the wall?" (*shadows*) "How can you make your shadow move in interesting ways? What shapes can you make with your shadow friend? Can you make your shadow dance with someone else's shadow?"

3. Continue to guide children in their shadow play as you transition them to the next activity.

Variations

Music and Movements: Change the type of music periodically to inspire different types of movement. Experiment with music from various cultures to see how the beat infuses children's movements.

Streamers and Scarves: Add a fun prop such as streamers or scarves. These make wonderful shadows as children move them in the light.

Sunny Day Shadows: Take children outside on a sunny day to play a game of shadow tag. In this game children have to tag one another's shadows instead of their bodies.

Cleanup Time

Often by February your usual cleanup-time songs and activities just aren't working anymore. Here are some new ones to add to your collection.

Skills and Concepts

- following directions
- large-motor development
- responsibility

What to Do

1. Sometimes children start cleaning well enough but don't stick with it. Use this song (right) to keep children actively involved from start to finish. Adapt line six, as well as the third and last lines of the refrain, to match your destination.

2. Repeat the song as needed for children to complete their cleanup.

Variation

 Sing a New Song: This song is also helpful to sing as children are cleaning because the words can be modified to go with whatever area children are picking up.

"The Pick-Up Song"
(sing to the tune of "Paw-Paw Patch")

Pick up blocks and put them on the shelf,
Pick up blocks and put them on the shelf,
Pick up blocks and put them on the shelf,
That's the way we clean up the blocks.

"I've Been Cleaning in the Classroom"
(sing to the tune of "I've Been Working on the Railroad")

I've been cleaning in the classroom
All the live-long day
I've been cleaning in the classroom
Just to pass the time away.
Can't you see we're almost finished?
Ready to go outside.
Can't you hear us all singing?
Cleaning side by side.

Teacher, can we go?
Teacher, can we go?
Teacher, can we go outside?
Teacher, can we go?
Teacher, can we go?
Can we go out to play?

Obstacle Course of the Imagination

Skills and Concepts

- using imagination
- creative movement
- relaxation
- large-motor development

Has cabin fever set in yet? In February the need for imaginative ways to move inside is strong. Children need to move their bodies but may not have enough opportunity to get outside. So take an imaginary trip to the playground to go through a pretend obstacle course!

 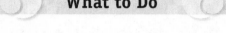 **What to Do**

1. Guide children through an imaginary obstacle course as you travel from one activity to another. Invite them to do their best pretending as you lead them over, around, and through different objects. A sample script follows.

   - *Let's pretend that we are going through an obstacle course at the gym. I will tell you where we are and what to do and you act it out right where you are. Okay? Great! Let's go!*

   - *First we need to walk to the playground. But here is our first obstacle. The classroom door is closed. How would you move if you were opening the door? Great! But now there is a big tube in our way. How would you move through it?*

   - *You did it! Now we can keep on walking. Oops, there is a giant ladder in front of us. How are we going to climb up and down the ladder? Excellent moving.*

2. Continue creating imaginary obstacles in your path until you reach your real or imaginary destination.

Variations

- **Collaborative Course:** Invite individual children to volunteer to lead the class in a segment of the obstacle course.

- **Ski, Hike, Swim:** Guide children on a pretend skiing trip, a hike in the woods, or a swim in the ocean. Think of obstacles that they might meet in each setting and include these in the activity.

Gone With the Wind

They say the winds of March come in like a lion and go out like a lamb. Use the lion-like March winds to inspire creative movement from one activity to another and calm the group into little lambs!

Skills and Concepts

• creative movement
• small- and large-motor development
• using imagination

What to Do

1. Give children paper streamers or cloth scarves. Play some light and flowing instrumental music and invite children to make the streamers flutter as though in the wind. Provide enough space for children to be able to move freely without bumping into one another.

2. As children move, describe both fierce lion-like winds and soft lamb-like winds. Encourage children to experiment with high and low, fast and slow windy movements.

3. When you're ready to move children on to the next activity, have them proceed together, first in a lion-like wind and then in a lamb-like wind, until they arrive calmly at their destination.

Variations

Windy Leader: Invite a transition leader to be the "wind." Have this child lead the class to its destination, acting out different kinds of winds for the class to follow.

Stop and Start: Play a noncompetitive musical chairs–like game to excuse children to the next activity. Have children move to the music. When you stop the music, they need to freeze in place. At this time, excuse two or more children and have them flutter away in a lamb-like wind. Start the music again for free movement. The next time you stop the music, have a few more children flutter away. Continue starting and stopping the music until all the children are gone with the wind!

Trees and Mountains

Revisit the yoga-like movements introduced in February (see Cats and Dogs, page 136), this time enjoying some fresh air as you take an imaginary trip to the mountains!

Skills and Concepts

- listening
- following directions
- using imagination
- large-motor development

What to Do

1. Have children start by standing tall with their feet together. Model how to pull shoulders back and down and place arms to the side with palms facing in. Tell children that this is called mountain pose because they are standing strong and tall like a high mountain.

2. Have children take several deep breaths through their nose. You might say, "Hold this position as you breathe deeply through your nose. I will count 1-2-3-4 for the in breath and 1-2-3-4 for the out breath." Count several times so children experience the strength of standing in this pose.

3. Now invite children to be a tree on the mountain! Guide them by saying, "Now we are going to be a tree on the mountain. Lift your right foot and place it against your calf. Let your right knee open out like a big branch. Choose a point on the floor to look at as you do this. It will help you keep your balance. Breathe in and out for the count of 1-2-3-4. Now place your foot on the floor and rest."

4. Repeat with the other foot.

Teaching Tip

Many of the simple yoga postures resemble things in nature. Try these poses to support children's healthy posture and relaxation.

Variations

🌀 **Going Further:** Once children feel comfortable in the tree pose with their foot on their calves, invite them to place their foot higher up on their leg. They can do this near a wall for balance. Remind children to look at a point on the floor to assist with balance. Children can also practice raising their arms over their heads in various positions to resemble giant branches.

🌀 **In the Forest:** Try being trees together. Have children stand side by side and gently lock arms. Have children lift their outside legs into tree pose and put the palms of their outside arms together in front. They can help each other balance!

Hokey Pokey Your Way Out

By March, children are confident in many of the songs they sing and are ready to have fun with something new. Here's a new version of a familiar favorite to create an interesting and active transition game for moving children place to place.

Skills and Concepts

- listening
- following directions
- large-motor development
- creative thinking

What to Do

1. Gather children in a circle (standing). Ask: "Who knows the song 'Hokey Pokey'? Can we sing one verse of it together?"

2. After singing a verse of the original song, teach children new words to sing to the same melody. Explain that they need to listen carefully because the song starts off the same way but changes along the way. Tell them to also listen for their names.

"Hokey Pokey Your Way Out"
(sing to the tune of "Hokey Pokey")

You put your hands in
You put your hands out.
You put your hands in
And shake them all about.
You do the hokey pokey
And turn yourself around.
[Child's name] and [child's name], go out!

[Repeat for head, feet/legs, whole self.]

Variations

My Way to Move: As children move away from the circle and off to the next activity, they can continue to "shake all about" the body part that was used in their verse.

More Parts to Move: Each time you play, invite children to suggest different body parts to put in the circle. They can do left and right hand, left and right foot, arms and legs!

The Surprise Bag Dilemma

Have you ever noticed how children respond to revisiting an activity presented in a new way? They delight in recognizing the familiar while exploring the new. Applying skills in a new context helps children build confidence in their abilities and discover new ideas. In this reversed version of December's Look at This! activity (page 129), children guess what is hiding in a surprise bag. This is an excellent way to introduce a new toy or material to the classroom and then transition into using it at activity time.

Skills and Concepts

- observing
- predicting
- vocabulary development
- deductive and inductive reasoning

What to Do

1. Place a new classroom material in a bag, without revealing the item to children.

2. Provide children with descriptive clues about its appearance and use. You might say, "Let's see if you can guess what new toy is hiding in the surprise bag. It is bouncy and red." Children might suggest a ball or a balloon. Provide another clue—for example, "It is bouncy and red and it rolls!"

3. Let children revise their guesses, and then reveal the contents of the bag.

Teaching Tip

This is a quick activity to do when you have some waiting time to fill. Just keep a surprise bag on hand and throw anything in it to play the guessing game. Here are some great things to hide in your surprise bag:

- Storytime books (give character and story clues to guess the book!)
- Pictures of nursery rhyme characters
- Rhythm instruments
- Alphabet letter blocks, tiles, or magnets
- Objects to introduce a new theme
- Props for dramatic play and storytelling
- Outdoor play toys, such as hoops and magnifiers

Variations

- **Time for a Surprise:** Use surprise bags during activity time, snack time, and even on your way outdoors to the playground. Children's attention will stay focused on putting clues together to determine the mystery object.

- **Surprise for Everyone:** Use the surprise bag technique as a way to pass out classroom materials without fights, since children have to accept the "luck of the draw."

Row Your Partner!

Cooperative activities are an essential part of March. Children are now comfortable enough with one another to be able to share a partner game that can lead into a transition to another activity.

Skills and Concepts

- cooperating
- large-motor development
- taking turns
- following directions

What to Do

1. Introduce the activity by singing "Row, Row, Row Your Boat" together. You might ask, "How could you row your boat with a partner? Find a partner and sit down on the floor across from each other. Can you put your hands on your partner's shoulders and start to row back and forth together by taking turns leaning forward?" Demonstrate how to do this, and let children experiment with this movement.

2. Singing to the tune of "Row, Row, Row Your Boat" again, have children repeat the movement, this time changing the words:

   Row, row, row as one.
   Just the two of you.
   Row, row, row as one.
   One plus one makes two.

3. After children have completed the game, you can excuse each twosome to the next activity with this verse:

   Go, go, go you two
   Go to the next place.
   Go, go, go you two
   With smiles on your faces.

Variations

 More Ways to Move: Ask children to suggest other ways they can move together with their partners. For example, can they sway side to side or roll around and around?

 Side by Side: Rather than hold each other's shoulders to row, children can sit side by side with their partners and each "hold an oar." Can they row their boat together, each pulling an oar through the water at the same time?

April Fool's Fun

It's hard to say where and when April Fool's Day started, but some say it was created as an expression of the giddiness of spring. Celebrate the first day of April with an April Fool's Day finger play. Children will love the silly fun of the rhymes and will delight in adding their own sillies to the mix!

Skills and Concepts

- following directions
- small-motor development
- listening
- creative thinking

What to Do

1. Begin by reciting the rhyme below several times with children.

2. Repeat the rhyme, this time guiding children in following along with the movements indicated.

3. Let children take turns creating new verses. Recite the first two lines together, and then let a volunteer suggest something new to complete line three ("It's a/an _____"). Children then recite the remaining two lines of the verse together.

"April Fool's"

Oh, wow!	[Children wide-eyed, cover their mouths.]
That looks cool.	[Children point.]
It's an elephant	[Children use arms to make an elephant trunk.]
In the school!	
April Fool's!	[Children look surprised.]

Oh, wow!	[Children wide-eyed, cover their mouths.]
That looks cool.	[Children point.]
It's a giant cake	[Children pretend to eat a piece of cake.]
In the school!	
April Fool's!	[Children look surprised or disappointed.]

Oh, wow!	[Children wide-eyed, cover their mouths.]
That looks cool.	[Children point.]
It's a crawling bug	[Children use fingers to show a bug crawling.]
In the school!	
April Fool's!	[Children look surprised.]

Variations

🌀 **Simple Substitutions:** Invite children to help you create a new rhyme structure to follow. As with the original rhyme, children can easily create new verses by simply substituting new words in line three. Here's an example to get you started:

> Oh, dear.
> It is clear.
> It's a banana
> In your ear!
> April Fool's!

🌀 **More Fun With Words:** Once children get the idea of this April Fool's game they will enjoy making up their own rhymes. Remember that at this stage it is not necessary for their finger play to rhyme or even be funny. The goal is for them to experiment with words for improbable situations.

We're Moving!

When it's spring and time to move outdoors, take a simple song based on a familiar tune along with you.

What to Do

1. You probably won't need much to inspire children to move outside, but a song can certainly help organize the process. A simple, familiar tune with repeating phrases makes this song an instant classic for moving children from one place to another.

"We're Moving"
(sing to the tune of "She'll Be Coming Around the Mountain")

We're moving to the playground
Go line up.
We're moving to the playground
Go line up.
We're moving to the playground
We're moving to the playground
We're moving to the playground
Go line up.

2. After practicing this verse with children a few times, replace the word *Go* in lines 2, 4, and 8 with children's names (a different one in each line)—for example, "We're moving to the playground, Sue, line up...." Have children get in line as they hear their name called.

Skills and Concepts

- listening
- singing
- creative movement
- large-motor development

Variations

- **More Than One:** Rather than replace the word *Go* with children's names, change lines 5, 6, and 7 to accommodate children's names:

  Sue and James to the playground
  Sue and James to the playground
  Sue and James to the playground
  Go line up.

- **Change the Words:** The simplicity of this song makes it easy to change the words and motions frequently. This will keep interest high and will involve children in the process as they apply creative thinking skills. For example, children can add a verse about what they will do in the playground: "We're going to the swing set. Give a push."

- **Add Movements:** Invite children to suggest different animal movements to use with the song—for example, "We're moving like an tiger. Here me roar!"

The Mystery Word Box

What happens when you reverse brainstorming? You get a guessing game–style transition activity that uses many words to find one! This is a quick thinking activity to use when you need something to fill waiting time.

Skills and Concepts

- vocabulary development
- descriptive language
- brainstorming
- deductive and inductive reasoning

What to Do

1. In advance of transition time, write a word on a large file card that relates to something children are familiar with. Use words for things that are easy to describe, such as weather, season, animals, or foods. Place the card in a mystery box.

2. Give children clues about the word—for example, if the mystery word is *rain*, give words such as *water*, *drop*, *puddle*, and *umbrella*. Write the clue words on chart paper and add a simple drawing when possible to illustrate each.

3. After each new clue word is given, review previous clues. You might say, "Let's read all the words we have collected. Can you think of something that all these words describe?"

4. Continue to provide clues until children guess the word.

Teaching Tip

Following are some mystery words and clues that work well with this game:

ice cream: cold, sweet, creamy, flavors

cat: fur, pointed, ears, claws, purrs, furry tail

tree: trunk, branches, leaves, bark

airplane: wing, propellers, flies

sun: warm, bright, star, s

Variations

 Collaborative Story: Another day, use the mystery word and clue words to write a class story. If desired, copy each sentence (or groups of sentences) onto a sheet of paper for children to illustrate. Bind to make a book.

Mystery Word Center: Copy clue words and pictures onto cards. Place the set of cards (mystery word plus clues) at a center for children to explore on their own.

All Aboard the Transition Train!

With the playful feeling of spring in the air, children will love to get moving as they climb aboard the Transition Train on the way to who knows where! Children will have to listen carefully in this game, because this time, instead of listening for their name to be called for the transition, they listen for physical characteristics as they are called.

Skills and Concepts

- listening
- following directions
- deductive reasoning
- vocabulary development

What to Do

1. Choose an attribute by which to call children to line up (or to excuse them to another activity). For example, you might call children by the first letter of their name, the number of letters in their name, or a favorite ice cream flavor. Sing a song to call children up by this attribute:

"Transition Train"
(sing to the tune of "Here We Go 'Round the Mulberry Bush")

Climb aboard the Transition Train
Transition Train, Transition Train
Climb aboard the Transition Train
If [describe the attribute, such as "your name starts with *m*"].

2. When children hear the attribute called that pertains to them, they climb aboard the train that you are leading. Children can join hands to create a train that winds its way through the classroom and eventually out the door!

Variations

🚂 **All Aboard:** When the train is ready to depart (all children are in line), sing a new verse as the train heads to its destination:

We're riding on the Transition Train
Transition Train, Transition Train
We're riding on the Transition Train
Going [add your destination here].

🚂 **Field Trip Train:** This activity works well for field trips, too. Just change the words to the "Field Trip Train" instead!

Silly Talk

Sometimes the best way to get the sillies out is to talk them out. Here is a great game to play when you have some waiting time to fill or you need to give children a creative outlet for their sillies.

Skills and Concepts

- creative expression
- focusing attention
- taking turns

What to Do

1. Start this activity by talking gibberish to the children. Just make up words and sounds but use them to speak with children very purposefully. It is best to have something in mind as you speak. For example, you might be talking about something you see out the window or something children will be doing. Use gestures to add meaning and be expressive. But avoid using words in English! One thing is for sure, you will definitely have children's attention.

2. Invite children to pick up on your silly talk by responding in their own gibberish to what you are saying.

3. After you have had this silly conversation, invite children to guess what you were talking about. You might ask, "What do you think I was talking about? What were some clues?"

4. Have children find partners and carry on silly conversations with each other. You might at first provide direction—for example, suggesting they make up words and sounds to tell each other something about themselves. Have them see if they can guess what the other is saying.

Variations

Walk and Talk: Let children continue their silly conversations as they transition together (in pairs) to an activity outside the classroom—for example, as they walk together to the lunchroom.

Nonsense Words: Take the game one step further by having children make up the world's longest nonsense word. Write it on chart paper and read it back to them. Then ask the group to explain what the word means. Descriptive words work best. Something can be so good that it is "celebratioussalliatioussuperduper" good!

Dance the Maypole

Skills and Concepts

• large-motor development
• cooperating

Many cultures celebrate the return of spring-like weather on May 1. This is traditionally a time of honoring the return of light and the growth of new life. A common activity for children around the world is the maypole dance. Use this version to provide movement breaks during transition times this month.

What to Do

1. Use a broomstick or a long dowel as your maypole. Attach very long and flowing colorful streamers to the top of the pole. Make sure there is a streamer for each child.

2. Stand with the pole in the center of an open space inside or outside the room. Hold the pole above your head so that the streamers fall down to the ground around you.

3. Tell children, "I want each of you to take a streamer and form a circle around the pole and me! When I start singing you can dance around the pole in the same direction and watch the colored streamers wrap around and around the pole. When you can't go any further, I'll give you the signal and you'll start dancing around the other way!"

Variations

Sing a Maypole Song: Sing a song together as children dance around the maypole.

"Maypole Song"
(sing to the tune of "Here We Go 'Round the Mulberry Bush")

Here we go 'round the pretty maypole,
The pretty maypole,
The pretty maypole.
Here we go 'round the pretty maypole,
On the first of May [or "In the May sunshine"].

Add a Twist: You can add some fun to the game by spinning around in the opposite direction to which children are going. What happens?

Wake Up, Earth!

How do you wake up the earth? With a bunch of stomping and dancing and a whole lot of noise! It is the tradition in some cultures to create noisy, stomping dances in May to wake up the earth and welcome spring. Morris or clog dancers use heavy footsteps, loud claps, ringing bells, and banging boards to give the earth a wakeup call. You can invite your children to do it, too! This activity is a good choice when children need a movement break during the day.

Skills and Concepts

- creative movement
- large-motor development
- cooperating

 ## What to Do

1. Explain to children, "The earth has been sleeping all winter and now that it is May it is time for it to wake up. Let's create a dance to wake up the earth! What kinds of foot movements can you do to wake up the earth? What can you do with your hands? The earth is sleeping deeply so we have to make lots of noise!"

2. Go outside together and invite children to dance as you play a strong drumbeat. You can also bring out recorded music with a lively beat to inspire their movements.

3. Eventually, pass out instruments and let children use these to add to their wakeup call.

4. All good things come to an end and this activity needs an ending, too. Use a signal to stop the action, and tell children that it worked! Take children over to a place where there is a plant just peaking up out of the earth or a place where you have hidden a bag of carrot sticks for all to share. Welcome, spring!

Variation

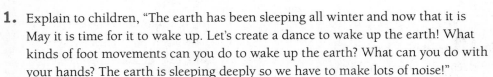

- **Wakeup Spring Chant:** Children may like to create a wakeup spring chant to go with their movements. Here is one to get you started:

Wake up, spring.
Wake up, spring.
With a step and a stomp,
And a clap, clap, clap,
Wake up, spring!

Pantomime Time

While May can be a time that inspires exuberant action, it is also good to balance this with quiet play. Use this creative pantomime game throughout the month to provide quiet action breaks, time fillers, or creative interludes.

Skills and Concepts

- creative movement
- problem solving
- deductive reasoning
- small- and large-motor development

What to Do

1. Explain that you are going to act out a word for children to guess. Choose a theme or category for your word to help children focus their thinking.

2. Model the activity by acting out a word that relates to the theme—for example, if your topic is "playground," you might act out being on a swing. Let children guess your word.

3. Have children take turns acting out other words within the topic. If you've exhausted the topic and have more time, choose a new topic and continue.

Teaching Tip

You might provide picture cards that correspond to various topics to help children choose words to act out.

Variations

- **Clowning Around:** Invite children to pretend to be clowns. Explain that some clowns don't talk! Invite children to have a clown "conversation" with a partner using movements and gestures instead of words! Can they guess what the other is communicating?

- **Favorite Authors:** Choose a favorite author, such as Tomie dePaola, as a topic. Take turns acting out favorite characters or scenes for others to guess.

Take a Walking Field Trip

Skills and Concepts

· listening

· observing

· predicting

· evaluating

An important part of spring is field study. But you don't have to go far to create a field trip. Consider adding mini–field trip "walks" to your transition activities. These are great activities for inspiring scientific thinking in a short period of time.

What to Do

1. When you have a short period of time to fill, and a need to have children use up a little extra energy, take a mini walk that focuses on separate senses. A "touch walk" would be to explore the textures around them, a "listening walk" to explore sounds. Focus a "looking walk" on a separate and specific topic such as trees, clouds, puddles, shadows, flowers, or birds. By choosing a singular focus, you invite children to become more focused explorers and invite them to consider what they see more deeply.

2. As you walk together, invite children to share observations they make using the specified sense. Children will be learning and using essential science concepts and process skills.

Variations

🌀 **Record Keeping:** Bring along a camera or a tape recorder to record children's findings. Children can revisit their walk later, using the pictures or tape recording as a springboard to writing or storytelling activities.

🌀 **Weather Walks:** Don't forget to include weather in your walking field trips. A windy-day walk is very different from a sunny-day walk. And there are amazing things to be found on an after-the-rain walk. Encourage children to compare observations of different kinds of weather.

The Mixed-Up Animal Game

All this springtime air can get everyone mixed up, including the animals! Here is a fun movement game to play together that doubles as a way to assign transition partners for the day.

Skills and Concepts

- matching
- creative movement
- cooperating

What to Do

1. Glue pictures of animals (from old magazines) on cardboard. Show children the pictures, and invite them to name the animals they see.

2. Cut the pictures in half (sideways). Now show children the picture parts in random order. Explain that the object of the game is to create a new animal by combining different halves.

3. Shuffle the cards and give one to each child. Select music to play, and explain that when you start the music children can move around the room. When the music stops, children need to find a partner with a different animal card. Partners then combine their animal halves to make silly creatures.

4. Have partners give their creatures a name and discuss how it moves. Play the music again and have children move like their new creature. Repeat several times so children get to make and move like a variety of mixed-up creatures!

5. When you're ready to transition children to the next activity, stop the music one last time, and have children find a partner to create and move like one more mixed-up creature. You might say, "This is your transition creature for the day. Whenever it is transition time you need to find your partner and move like your creature from one activity to another. How does it move? Let's try it as we go to [destination]."

Variations

🔵 **All About My Mixed-Up Creature:** During activity time, place art and writing materials at a center for children to draw pictures of and write about their mixed-up creatures. They might, for example, draw pictures of and label their creature's habitat or family members.

🔵 **More Mixed-Up Animals:** Stock a center with old magazines and workbooks that contain pictures of animals. Provide scissors, glue, and large index cards. Let children cut out pictures, glue them to cards, and cut them apart to make more mixed-up animals.

How We've Grown!

June is a time for children to reflect on how much they've grown during the year. You can incorporate this concept into your transition activities throughout the month. Try using this growing-up story as a settling-down or thought-provoking activity all month long. Each time children act out the stages of growing up as you tell the story, they will get more out of it.

Skills and Concepts

- creative movement
- using imagination
- listening
- reflecting
- small- and large-motor development

What to Do

1. Have children find a comfortable place to sit on the floor. Be sure children are not too close to one another. They will need to be able to move freely.

2. Introduce the activity by saying, "I am going to tell a pretend story of growing up. As I tell the story, you can use your body to act out the different ages." You can tell the following story, changing it as needed to fit the needs of your group or your own personality.

Growing Up

Take a deep breath and close your eyes. Can you remember being a tiny baby in your crib? If you can't remember, you can pretend! You are sleeping, and as you awake you lie on your back and wiggle your arms and legs. Do you see a mobile hanging above your crib? Try to gently kick it with your feet. Good. Now time has passed and you are getting bigger. You can roll over all by yourself! Soon you can pick up your head and look around. What do you see? Wow, look at that! You just rolled over onto your tummy for the first time! Now you are beginning to crawl very slowly and carefully. As you are out exploring one day, you discover that you can hold onto a chair and pull yourself up. What do you see? You pull yourself along on the furniture and take your first steps. Then, boom! You fall down but you get right back up again. You keep trying and very quickly you are walking! Look at you walk and walk. Eventually, you start to run and skip just like you do now. So now let's skip our way to the next activity. You've grown into big kids now!"

Variations

 Picture Card Prompts: Create a set of picture cards that show basic stages of development that are described in the story. Have a volunteer use the picture cards to tell the "Growing Up" story as the other children act it out. As children become familiar with the story through repetition over time, they will be increasingly able to include details in their storytelling.

Baby Animals Grow Up: Invite children to pretend to be a baby animal—for example, a kitten. Adapt the story to guide them through the stages of growing up as this animal.

Nature's Treasure Hunt

Skills and Concepts

- observing
- comparing
- visual perception

Here is a special end-of-the-year transition activity you can take outside to your play area for a celebration of the senses. In this last treasure hunt of the year, children will take a cue from animals and create a camouflage treasure hunt together! As children locate an object that has been camouflaged, they can then move on to the next activity. (Or use as a way to line up children a few at a time.)

 ## What to Do

1. Take a nature walk (or use photos in books) to show children how some animals can hide on something that is the same color and/or texture as they are. For example, a green salamander might hide on a green leaf. A walking stick can hide on a stick. Introduce the word *camouflage* and discuss its meaning "a way of hiding that lets something or someone blend in with the surroundings."

2. Collect some items for children to camouflage. Invite children to suggest places they could camouflage the items. Try out some of their ideas and notice how the background camouflages each item. For example, a red crayon might be camouflaged on a reddish stone or brick because they're the same color.

3. Provide a new set of objects to camouflage. Have a few volunteers hide the items on a camouflaging background (while other children close their eyes). Then let children hunt for the objects, thinking about what sorts of places would make good hiding places and why. When children find an object, have them move on to the next activity (or line up if they are outside and heading indoors).

Teaching Tip

You might want to start this game inside and take it outside another day. This will give children more experience with the concept in a smaller and controlled space before taking it out to a larger one. Also, share children's books about camouflage—for example, *A Color of His Own* by Leo Lionni (Knopf, 2006) and *The Mixed-Up Chameleon* by Eric Carle (HarperCollins, 1984).

Variation

Yarn Worms: Cut yarn in different colors into strips about three inches each. Let children camouflage the yarn "worms" for others to find. Or, for each child, place a piece of yarn on something that is the same color. When it's time to line up, have children find a worm and then line up. Pass a basket down the line and have children drop in their worms, and then off you go.

Walk the Tightrope!

Has the coming summer vacation gotten your children overly excited? Try a tightrope movement game that both calms them down and channels their extra physical energy. They have to move quietly and carefully when walking on a tightrope because they don't want to fall off!

Skills and Concepts

- creative movement
- social interaction
- large-motor development

 ## What to Do

1. Create a pretend tightrope across the room or from one place to another. You can draw an imaginary line in the air or use tape to create an actual line on the floor.

2. Invite children to imagine that the line is stretched across a circus big top and they have to be very careful not to fall off as they tiptoe across it.

3. Add a song to make the game more fun. Here are two (at right) to try.

Variations

🌀 **More Ways to Move:** After children have conquered tiptoeing the tightrope, invite them to walk it backwards, on their knees, or on one foot.

🌀 **Tightrope Partners:** Tightrope walkers often have partners. Have children find a partner and walk the rope together. How many different ways can they move together without falling off?

"Tightrope Walker"
(sing to the tune of "Are You Sleeping?")

Tightrope walker
Tightrope walker
Don't fall down.
Don't fall down.

Tiptoe very slowly
Tiptoe very slowly
Spin around.
Spin around.

"Don't Look Down"
(sing to the tune of "London Bridge Is Falling Down")

Tightrope walker, don't look down
Don't look down, don't look down
Tightrope walker, don't look down
Tiptoe softly.

A Clothing Relay

Use this traditional field-day game as a fun way to transition children from one activity to another. It is challenging for both large and small muscles, and it can be used as an action break to help children use up some extra energy.

Skills and Concepts

- following directions
- small- and large-motor development

What to Do

1. Set up two piles of old clothes and hats at one end of the room or in an open area outside.

2. Have children form two lines about six to ten feet away from the piles. The object of the game is for children to run to a pile and put on one piece of clothing, and then run back and tag the next person in line.

3. This person then runs to the pile and puts on something else. Children continue in this way until they are all dressed in funny outfits.

4. In the second round, children take turns running back to where the pile was and taking off the costume. When they are finished, they can either sit down at the end by the pile of clothes and cheer for the others or go off to the next activity.

Variation

- **Freeze and Thaw:** Periodically throughout the game, stop the action by calling "Freeze!" Ask children to take a funny stance like a sculpture and look at one another. When the giggling has subsided, call out "Thaw" and tell children to go back to the relay game.

A Wizard's Spell

Skills and Concepts

• focusing attention
• creative expression

By June you need a few new tricks up your sleeve to get children to follow directions and listen. There is something about magic (even if it is pretend) that gets children's attention. Use these wizardly chants to focus children who have a case of too much end-of-the-year fever!

What to Do

1. Take a page from Harry Potter and use these wizard "spells" to get children looking at you and ready to go.

Abracadabra,
Pull your ear
Wiggle your fingers
And look up here!

Abracadabra,
Tickle your knee
Hands in your lap
And look at me!

2. When it's time to excuse children from the group, wave your wand and chant:

Abracadabra
Take a bow
Spin around
And go out now!

Variations

● **Special Effects:** For an extra-special effect, make a magic wand out of a paper towel tube and streamers. Children will enjoy taking turns as the wizard, too!

● **Wizardly Words:** Children will enjoy making up their own versions of the spells. Don't worry if they don't rhyme. They just have to have fun.